NEW YEAR, SAME YOU

Also by Geoff Tibballs

The Grumpy Old Git's Guide to Life

The Grumpy Old Git Quiz Book

NEW YEAR, SAME YOU

CHANNEL YOUR INNER GRUMP

GEOFF TIBBALLS

Michael O'Mara Books Limited

First published in Great Britain in 2019 by
Michael O'Mara Books Limited
9 Lion Yard
Tremadoc Road
London SW4 7NQ

A CIP catalogue record for this book is available from the British
Library.

Papers used by Michael O'Mara Books Limited are natural, recyclable
products made from wood grown in sustainable forests. The
manufacturing processes conform to the environmental regulations
of the country of origin.

ISBN: 978-1-78929-189-6 in hardback print format
ISBN: 978-1-78929-190-2 in ebook format

1 2 3 4 5 6 7 8 9 10

Illustrations by Andrew Pinder
Designed and typeset by D23
Printed and bound by CPI Group (UK) Ltd, Croydon CR0 4YY

www.mombooks.com

CONTENTS

INTRODUCTION

'To have a grievance is to have a purpose in life.'

ALAN COREN

At the start of every new year it's the same old story. In every newspaper, magazine or on every TV channel we are bombarded with suggestions on how to improve our apparently miserable lives. There are diet regimes to which we must strictly adhere if we are to have any hope of living to see next Christmas, fitness DVDs brought out by someone who finished fifth in a TV singing contest, and endless books on how changing our mindset and embracing positive thinking can enrich our future. You need to vent *more*, they say. I tried it, but you could still see my lips move.

And isn't positive thinking overrated? Has it ever achieved *anything* useful, like winning the lottery or getting a date with Elle Macpherson? Goliath was positive he could beat David in combat, but a fat lot of good it did him. And when it comes to the other recommendations by the wellness industry, do we really want to take up yoga at our age? What happens if we can't get up afterwards? As for meditation, we do that every day anyway, wondering where we put our car keys or what we came upstairs for. Meditation is just a prolonged, senior moment.

So what if this old dog doesn't want to be taught new tricks? What if he is perfectly happy the way he is – curled up in front of the fire for most of the day, breaking off only to take a nip out of a deserving ankle or to relieve himself on someone's immaculately ordered garden of mindfulness.

This book is for those who are happy to continue spreading grumpiness rather than channelling our inner Zen. It is for those of us who are comfortable in our own skin, even if it doesn't fit us anymore.

DON'T TELL ME NOT TO STRESS OUT!

Mindfulness gurus tell us that the key to enlightenment is to remain calm at all times. These people say that we must never act hastily or become stressed. These people say that while others may be running around frantically in a blind panic, we should sit down quietly and patiently and weigh up the best option. But have they ever been in an earthquake or chased by a crazed axeman?

'If you can keep your head while all around you are losing theirs, you probably haven't understood the seriousness of the problem.'

DAVID BRENT

The laws of mindfulness state that there are four steps to leading a better, more rewarding life:

Consideration for other people at all times, treating them the way you would wish to be treated yourself.
Recognizing that others have their own problems in life, even if they do not express them publicly.
Accepting that things may not always be perfect in your life and that you should resist trying to make them so.
Peace of mind represents the highest form of contentment.

Or just remember the acronym **CRAP**. Instead, follow these seven steps towards leading a happier life:

1. Don't leave the last biscuit in the packet for someone else; they won't thank you for it.

2. Never allow anyone else to become custodian – even temporarily – of the TV remote; they can't be trusted with such a vital piece of equipment.

3. Never go to bed angry. Stay awake and plot your revenge.

4. Don't take your worry to bed with you – make your partner sleep in the spare room.

5. Smile at totally random moments – those around you will start worrying about what you find so amusing.

6. Don't hate yourself in the morning – sleep till noon.

7. And don't read any articles about mindfulness.

Now that's clear, remember . . .

When you get home at the end of a stressful day, you do have choices. It is imperative that you take back control of your destiny as quickly as possible. Nobody can force you to do something against your will. You alone must decide which path to take, which will be most beneficial to your wellbeing. So, which is it going to be – the Pinot Gris or the Sauvignon Blanc?

A couple were talking one evening. 'Darling,' said the husband, 'I'm so sorry about my bad moods. I shouldn't take out my anger and frustration on you. I don't know how you manage to stay so calm around me.'

'I always go and clean the toilet when that happens,' she replied.

'And that helps?'

'Yes, because I use your toothbrush.'

'There's no panic like the panic you momentarily feel when your hand or head is stuck in something.'

PETER KAY

Never hypothetically ask yourself if the person in front of you can go any slower, because the answer is always yes.

A marriage counsellor was trying to ascertain his patient's state of mind by asking her some questions. He began: 'Did you wake up grumpy this morning?'

'No,' she answered. 'I let him sleep.'

PICK YOUR FIGHTS CAREFULLY

In the same way that other people have different things that bring joy to their lives, every grumpy old git will have something different that raises their hackles. It could be a certain TV presenter, a particular occupation (doctors' receptionists, bankers, lawyers and politicians to name but four) or a specific circumstance that puts us in a foul mood. We don't see ourselves as being naturally grumpy at all; we are all perfectly reasonable people who just happen to be victims of society. Perhaps there should be an organization – Grumblers Anonymous – where we can gather regularly to air our grievances with like-minded souls. Even though there are days when our blood boils almost as frequently as our kettle, it is important not to stress out over everything. There are times when it is definitely better to bite your lip.

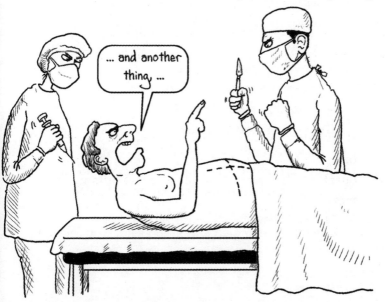

So again, remember, never argue with:

* a spouse who is packing your parachute
* anyone who is holding a bread knife or a pair of sharp scissors
* people in groups of four or more, especially if one is accompanied by a large dog on a chain
* 1diots – they will drag you down to their level and then beat you with experience
* and another reason for never arguing with idiots is that people watching might not be able to tell the difference

———

To mark an old man's one hundred and seventh birthday, the local newspaper despatched a reporter to interview him. The reporter was keen to know the secret of the old man's longevity.

'The secret to a long life,' revealed the old man, 'is never to argue with anyone.'

The reporter was incredulous. 'That's crazy,' she said. 'There must be something else, maybe diet or meditation, that has kept you so healthy for so long. You can't live to a hundred and seven simply by not arguing. It's not possible!'

The old man smiled at her and said: 'You know, you could be right.'

A husband confided to his friend that he was sick of the constant arguments with his wife. 'Every time we have a row she gets historical!'

'Don't you mean hysterical?' suggested the friend.

'No, I mean historical. Every argument we have, she'll say: "And don't think I've forgotten that time when you . . ."'

HEALTHY, DELICIOUS RETRIBUTION

Of all the growth industries in the twenty-first century, few have experienced a boom quite like fraud. Who would be surprised if 'Fraudstering' is soon offered as a career option in schools? It certainly offers more realistic prospects than media studies or sports psychology. Almost every other phone call you get these days seems to be from someone trying to rip you off, often a distant voice claiming to be your internet provider patiently explaining that your router, fortunately, has just alerted them to a significant fault which, if not dealt with immediately, will result in your internet connection being cut off forever and a plague of locusts descending on your head. Given that your internet provider couldn't give a toss either about your broadband speed or a connection that is jumpier than a naturist at a barbecue, the call is clearly a scam.

The wisdom you have accrued over the years means that you can usually detect a fraudster as soon as they open their mouth, but whereas in the past you probably just slammed the phone down on them – accompanied by a bellow of blazing words – now could be the time to adopt a more relaxed, considered approach that will be easier on your blood pressure.

COLD-CALLER
COPING MECHANISM – 1

Tell the caller that you need to fetch a pen and paper to write down the instructions and then leave them on hold while you make a cup of tea or do a spot of gardening. It is their time and money, so the chances are that by the time you eventually return to the phone they will have given up in frustration and will mark your number down as 'Never Ever Ring Again'.

An overly stressed man had been seeing a psychiatrist for three years in a bid to cure his irrational fear that there were monsters lurking under his bed. But all the psychiatrist's efforts were in vain and the man was no nearer to being cured. Eventually he decided that future sessions were a waste of time and money and so he cancelled the appointments.

A few weeks later, the psychiatrist bumped into the man in the street. The man was looking much happier.

'You look well,' remarked the psychiatrist.

'Yes,' smiled the man. 'That's because I'm cured. After all this time, I can finally go to sleep at night without worrying that there are monsters lurking under my bed.'

The psychiatrist was pleased but puzzled. 'How have you managed to get cured? Nothing I tried with you seemed to work.'

'I went to see a different doctor,' explained the man. 'He is a behaviourist and cured me in a single session.'

'In one session?!' exclaimed the psychiatrist. 'How?'

'It was simple,' said the man. 'He told me to saw the legs off my bed.'

———

A husband hadn't been feeling too well for months but, being a typical man, didn't want to trouble the doctors until finally his wife forced him to book an appointment at the health centre. After a thorough examination, the doctor revealed his diagnosis: the husband was, quite simply, stressed out.

'You'll need six months of total relaxation,' said the doctor as the agitated wife took out a notepad and began feverishly scribbling the orders for these months of relaxation.

'How should I go about it?' asked the husband. 'Do I need to take any tablets?'

'Not really,' said the doctor, 'but I'd like your wife to take one tranquillizer four times a day.'

———

THE STRESS TEST

Which of these are guaranteed to make you grumpy?

* Finding someone sitting in your reserved seat on a train, smirking.

* The last BLT sandwich being sold to the person before you in the queue.

* Pens that mysteriously disappear from your desk without leaving so much as a goodbye note.

* A shopper with one item too many in their basket in the supermarket express lane.

* Paintbrushes that moult mid-stroke like an alopecic budgie.

* Getting into an ice cold bath because the hot water ran out after two minutes.

* Children allowed to run amok in restaurants.

* Finding that the cost of your online flight tickets has come down by 20 per cent since you booked them.

* Duvet covers that ensnare you while you are trying to fit them, leaving only your pinkies poking out the bottom.

* Insurance company or funeral plan commercials on daytime TV that target anyone over the age of forty-five by promising them 'peace of mind'.

* Toothbrush packaging that has no obvious point of entry.

* People reading over your shoulder.

* Only leaving the house for five minutes but finding on your return that a courier attempted to deliver the parcel you've been waiting two months for.

* Socks that suddenly decide they're happier being single.

* Small, yapping dogs.

If the answer is all of them, relax. You're NORMAL, there's no need to change your ways. Stay free, stay true, stay grumpy.

———

A woman arrived home to find that her house had been ransacked. Drawers had been emptied and clothes were strewn everywhere, but she didn't report it as a break-in until the following day. When a police officer called round to investigate, he asked her the reason for the delay.

She said: 'To be perfectly honest, Officer, I didn't know I'd been robbed. My husband went away yesterday on business, so when I saw the place in such a state, I simply assumed he had lost one of his socks again.'

COLD-CALLER COPING MECHANISM – 2

When the caller begins by asking how you are today, instead of replying suspiciously 'Fine, thanks', launch into a litany of woe detailing your various personal and health problems. Describe each one in painstaking detail without letting the caller get a word in and you'll soon find that your irritable bowel is in good company.

GRUMPINESS MOTTOS

Some are really worth living by. Try these:

* You're not grumpy at all – it's just that other people are recklessly happy.

* No problem is so big or complicated that you can't run away from it.

* Keep the dream alive. Hit the snooze button.

* If someone hits you in the face, turn the other cheek. That way the swelling is even.

* Never go to sleep on an argument – a mattress is much more comfortable.

* Always be prepared to let go – unless you're bungee jumping.

* Don't tire yourself out by seeking answers to the impossible – nobody else knows what turkey ham is either.

* When someone says to you 'Have a nice day', tell them you have other plans.

* If you want to forget all your troubles, buy a pair of tight shoes.

* The meek may inherit the earth, but they won't get that pothole in the street outside your house repaired.

* If you can smile when things go wrong, you probably have someone in mind to blame.

* A problem shared is a buck passed.

* Sure, you can't take it with you but you can hide it where no other bastard can find it.

* Open yourself up to the many paths available in life, and then take the easiest.

* Let go of your mind. You probably lost it years ago anyway.

* Look out for number one, and don't step in number two.

* On the keyboard of life, always keep one finger on the escape key.

* Life's a bitch. Deal with it. Just accept that some days you're the pigeon, some days you're the statue.

———————

Show me a man who has both feet on the ground and I'll show you a man who can't put on his trousers.

COLD-CALLER
COPING MECHANISM – 3

Turn the tables on the caller by pre-recording your own music and putting them on hold while you take your time in fetching the necessary documents. Place it right next to the phone and start with something gentle before blaring out Motorhead or Megadeth at full blast. They will soon get the message.

A young woman turned to her fiancé and said: 'When we get married, I want to share all your troubles and worries.'

'That's very kind of you, darling,' he replied, 'but I don't have any troubles or worries.'

She said: 'Well, that's because we're not married yet.'

———

'Life is like a sewer. What you get out of it depends on what you put into it.'

TOM LEHRER

———

'I believe you should live each day as if it was your last, which is why I don't have any clean laundry, because who wants to wash clothes on the last day of their life?'

JACK HANDEY

———

'Just squeeze your rage up into a bitter little ball and release it at an appropriate time, just like that day I hit the referee with the whisky bottle.'

HOMER SIMPSON, *THE SIMPSONS*

———

A man had just stepped out of his house and was approaching his car when he noticed two youngsters trying to force open the passenger door. Defying his advancing years, he chased them down the street, caught them and pinned them against a wall. As the kids began to tremble, he raised his fists but then said: 'Boys, this is your lucky day. I'm going to let you go. But don't let me catch you around here again.'

The boys ran off and a neighbour who had witnessed the confrontation went over to the man. 'I'm impressed,' he said. 'The old Henry would have battered those two to a pulp. You really have changed your ways.'

'Not really,' said the man. 'But I'm on my way to my anger management class and I didn't think it would look good if I turned up with blood on my shirt.'

LIVE EACH DAY . . .

A familiar mindfulness mantra is live each day as if it were your last, although telling yourself that you're going to die within the next twenty-four hours hardly matches the attitude of positive thinking that they're always emphasizing. But if you reckon you're about to peg it:

* Only buy one toilet roll at a time.

* Don't bother recording any of the following day's TV shows.

* Send an abusive email to anyone who has ever annoyed you. That may take most of your day.

* Try to sell your diary and calendar on eBay.

* Don't waste money on getting your haircut. The funeral parlour will do it for you.

TRIED MEDITATION?

Worried about his stress levels at work, a businessman decided to join a meditation class. With everyone gathered around in a circle, the meditation teacher turned to him and said quietly but firmly: 'I want you to take three deep, slow breaths . . . and then very slowly . . . let go of your mobile phone.'

Sitting around all day doing nothing

Meditating

Two old acquaintances bumped into each other in the street . . .

'How are you?' asked one.

'I'm fine, thanks,' said the other.

'How's your son? Has he got himself a job yet?'

'No, but he has started meditating.'

'Meditating. What's that?'

'I don't know, but it's better than sitting around all day doing nothing.'

———

The only good thing about meditation is you can do it sitting down.

Q: Why did the meditation teacher give no change when a student paid for a meditation cushion?

A: Because change has to come from within.

Q: Why are meditation teachers uncomfortable around vacuum cleaners?

A: Because there are too many attachments involved.

MINDFULNESS V GRUMPINESS

There are always at least two ways of looking at life. I'm not saying which of these is better . . . just that I know which side I'm on!

M: Feelings come and go like clouds in a windy sky.

G: But what if they are nimbus clouds and you get drenched?

M: A smile costs nothing.

G: Unless it's while a judge is sentencing you, in which case it could cost you an extra six months for contempt of court.

M: Three things cannot hide for long: the Moon, the Sun and the Truth.

G: What about my glasses? I haven't been able to find them for three weeks!

M: Your actions are your only true belongings.

G: That's what the airline company tried to tell me when they lost my baggage last year.

M: Nothing can harm you as much as your own thoughts unguarded.

G: I think a lion might come close.

M: If you are facing in the right direction, all you need to do is keep on walking.

G: Not a good idea if you live by the sea.

M: Fear is a natural reaction to moving closer to the truth.

G: Particularly if you have buried a body under the patio.

M: Life is better when we don't try to do everything.

G: So think how much better it will be if we do nothing.

M: Friends come and go like the waves of the ocean.

G: Except the really dull ones who cling to you like limpets.

M: One who is patient glows with an inner radiance.

G: One who is a patient glows with an inner rage because his operation has been cancelled at the last minute.

M: The most precious gift we can offer others is our presence.

G: Great, that will save money at birthdays and Christmas.

COLD-CALLER
COPING MECHANISM – 4

Pretend that the person the caller wants to speak to has recently been murdered and that you are a detective at the crime scene. Ask them a series of probing questions regarding their connection to the 'deceased' and say that you will probably need to interview them formally at the police station. They will quickly hang up, never to pester you again.

M: It's always darkest before dawn.

G: So if you're going to steal your neighbour's milk, that's the time to do it.

M: It is never too late to turn on the light.

G: That's all very well, but you don't have to pay my energy bills.

M: Wherever you go, I will be there beside you.

G: That's called stalking.

Q: Why did the stressed husband go potholing?
A: Because he tended to cave under pressure.

If you can keep your head while others around you are losing theirs, you may want to land your helicopter somewhere else.

————

And remember, although you may not suffer from stress yourself, you could be a carrier.

2

TAKE MORE EXERCISE? JOG ON!

At our age we no longer refer to our knees as right and left but as good and bad. We can remember when we used to be the hare but now we struggle to keep pace with the tortoise. We can achieve the same degree of fatigue experienced at the end of a strenuous hour-long workout at the gym just by getting up out of a chair suddenly. Where once we used to rock around the clock, now it's a slow walk around the block. Yet health experts constantly badger us to exercise more, to kick off the New Year with a fitness regime. In truth, for most grumpy old gits, pushing sixty is exercise enough.

> *'Whenever I feel like exercise, I lie down until the feeling passes.'*
> ROBERT M. HUTCHINS

WORRIED YOU'RE NOT GETTING ENOUGH?

When somebody tells you that you ought to exercise more, your immediate reaction is usually something along the lines of: 'What do you mean? I get plenty of exercise.' To underline your point, you proceed to list your weekly activities, leaving no stone unturned. First, you climb out of bed, which, with your bodyweight, equates to heavy lifting. Next you have to bend down to put your socks on – one on each foot – a classic toe-touching workout. Then there are two descents and one ascent of the stairs, which, given the climb, is surely tougher than being on a treadmill at the gym. Finally, setting off for work, you walk five yards to your car, which, allowing for return trips at both ends of your commute five days a week, amounts to a hundred yards. If you're late, this walk is so brisk that it could almost be considered a trot, so effectively you're running a hundred yards. But if you're worried you're not getting enough exercise, check if:

* You get exhausted just winding your watch.

* Your idea of exercise is to sit in the bath tub, pull the plug and fight the current.

* Your only exercise on holiday is sucking in your stomach every time you see a bikini.

* The only yoga stretch you've perfected is the yawn.

* Even your double chin has a double chin.

* Your knees buckle but your belt won't.

* You're so unfamiliar with the gym that you call it James.

* You have flabby thighs, but fortunately your stomach covers them.

* You sit in a rocking chair and can't get it going.

* Your chief form of exercise over the past few years has been getting over the hill.

* You think breakfast in bed counts as a morning workout.

* Although no man is an island, you are so overweight that you come pretty close.

* When you drop something, instead of picking it up you think to yourself: 'Do I really need it?'

* When you drop something, you don't pick it up until your shoelaces need tying.

* The only exercise you get is jumping to conclusions.

———

A husband snapped grumpily to his wife: 'What have you been doing with all the grocery money I give you every week?'

She said: 'Turn sideways and look in the mirror.'

FITNESS – SCHMITNESS

So which of these apply to you?

* Don't think of yourself as being fat, think of yourself as being a well-rounded individual.

* Don't think of yourself as being fat, think of yourself as being easier to see.

* If God had wanted us to touch our toes, he would have put them on our knees.

* At our age, we get enough exercise just by pushing our luck.

* When you were younger, you looked forward to getting up early to exercise. Now getting out of bed in the morning *is* your exercise.

* The only advantage of exercising every day is you die healthier.

* Don't think of yourself as being fat: think of yourself as being hard to kidnap.

* Mindfulness says that exercise feels best after it is finished. But it feels better still if it's not even started.

* Old people are more vulnerable in winter, so that extra layer around the middle can protect you against the bitter cold.

* Thinking that letting your mind wander counts as exercise.

* If your doctor tells you that you need to get in shape, politely remind him that round is a shape.

* According to mindfulness, you've only got one body but in your case you've probably ruined it already.

* Learn to accept that the only way you'll ever have a smokin' hot body is to be cremated.

* Treat your body as if it were a temple, even though there are no worshippers.

* The older you get, the tougher it is to lose weight, because by then your body and your fat have become really good friends.

* Don't think of it as having a beer gut. Think of it as having a protective covering for your rock-hard abs.

* Exercise your mind the same as you would exercise your body – once a week and only if it's not raining.

*'I try to keep fit. I've got these parallel bars at home.
I run at them and try to buy a drink from
both of them.'*

ARTHUR SMITH

Two men in their fifties were chatting at the bar. 'I have to say,' said one, 'you're in good shape for your age. I wish I could lose some of my belly flab. What's your secret?'

The other replied: 'I definitely owe my athletic physique to my wife and clean living – clean the car . . . Clean the attic . . . Clean the garage.'

———

A grumpy old git was standing in front of the mirror admiring his six-pack. But then it started to get warm, so he put it back in the refrigerator.

———

You can't always help it if you don't get enough strenuous exercise; it might walk in your family.

GRUMPY OLD LAZINESS

Let's be honest, some of us are so idle that the only time we kick into action is when we see that our phone battery is down to 10 per cent. In fact, if there were an award for laziness ... we'd probably send someone else to pick it up. But is laziness such a bad thing? Instead let's think of it as conserving energy. Let's kick off with a couple of quotes:

'My idea of exercise is a good brisk sit-down.'

PHYLLIS DILLER

'I believe that every human has a finite amount of heartbeats. I don't intend to waste any of mine running around doing exercises.'

NEIL ARMSTRONG

———

And then learn the Big 8:

1. Don't think of yourself as being lazy: think of yourself as a relaxaholic.

2. If a thing's worth doing, it would have been done already.

3. Hard work pays off in the future; laziness pays off now.

4. Hard work has never hurt anyone, but it's not worth taking the chance.

5. Progress is made by lazy people looking for an easier way to do things.

6. Your future depends on your dreams. So don't waste any time, stay in bed all day.

7. There's no excuse for laziness but I'm working on it.

8. And if someone has the temerity to suggest that all you've done is sit around for hours drinking beer, point out that you have made three round trips to the fridge to fetch another beer and that these cans don't open themselves. Never underestimate the amount of exercise involved in opening a can of beer. Some of those ring pulls put up quite a fight.

Rabbits hop all day, eat all their vegetables, but only live for five years; whales swim all day, eat fish and only drink water, but they are fat; and tortoises do absolutely *nothing* energetic but live for two hundred years. Think about it.

———

Q: How do you get a man to exercise?
A: Tie the TV remote to his shoelaces.

GRUMPY OLD GYM WORKOUTS

The latest fad is to have a personal fitness trainer. But why would you want to pay a stranger a ridiculous amount of money to tell you that you are a tubby when you can obtain exactly the same information by listening to the abuse you can get from a speak-your-weight machine?

Q: Why is the gym like a church?
A: No matter what you do all week, you think you can erase it all with just one visit.

Q: Why did the aerobics instructor cross the road?
A: Because some people on the other side were still able to walk.

Q: What is an easy way to add squats to your daily routine?
A: Move the beer to the bottom shelf of the fridge.

And is this training malarkey all it's cracked up to be?

* An exercise bicycle in your home soon becomes a really expensive coat hanger.

* As soon as you join a gym, you'll feel pounds lighter – in your pocket.

* The only difference between an aerobics instructor and a dentist is that the dentist lets you sit down while he hurts you.

* Aerobics – a series of strenuous exercises that help convert fats, sugars and starches into aches, pains and cramps.

* When your personal fitness trainer tells you to do ten press-ups, ask if they mean in sequence or can you can spread them over a few weeks.

———

A man was telling his neighbour about his first session at the gym. 'I found this great machine, but I only used it for an hour because I was starting to feel sick. It's really good though. It does everything: Snickers, Mars bars, M&Ms and crisps.'

———

Why is it that someone who does two hours of fitness workouts every day still needs to find the closest parking spot to the gym?

———

People who think they can run away from their problems have obviously never farted on a treadmill.

———

A man asked the gym trainer: 'I want to impress that beautiful girl. Which machine should I use?'

Answer: 'Try the ATM.'

———

Two women were passing a poster at their local gym that read: *Nothing is impossible!* One turned to the other and said: 'Yeah, except trying to cancel your gym membership!'

A man was attending his first aerobics class. The instructor said: 'Now I want you all to do twenty jumping jacks.'

The man put up his hand and said: 'Twenty jumping jacks is a lot for a beginner. So today can I just do half of that?'

'Okay, I suppose so,' said the instructor.

So the man stood still and clapped twenty times.

———

A man walked into his local bar and announced to his friend: 'I've just burned two thousand calories.'

'Really?' said the friend, sounding impressed.

'Yes, that's the last time I leave brownies in the oven while I take a nap.'

A man signed up for an exercise class and was told to wear loose-fitting clothes. He said: 'If I had any loose-fitting clothes, I wouldn't have needed to join!'

———

'I did thirty squats this morning,' said an old man to his friend.

'Wow! That's pretty good.'

'Yeah, but I still couldn't find my damned contact lens!'

GRUMPY OLD JOGGING

Why would anyone willingly choose to take up jogging? (Quick answer: to hear heavy breathing again.) I mean ... have you ever seen a happy jogger? They always look to be on the verge of a major cardiac event. Even at our age there are more pleasurable ways of getting red-faced, breathless and sweaty – and which don't play havoc with your verrucas. And then there are the shorts.

Now, a pair of shorts is perfectly acceptable attire if you're young and have got reasonable legs but on men of a certain age ... If you're fairly slim, shorts either make you look like a Boy Scout who has seen better days or an item of Chippendale furniture. So if someone says you look like a Chippendale, they're not necessarily being

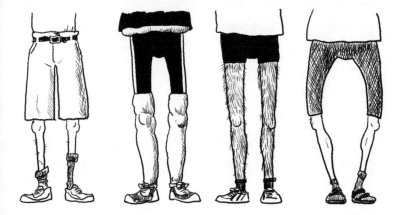

complimentary. And if you're overweight – which is probably why you need to jog – shorts simply accentuate the fact. You may look as if you need stabilisers.

It's okay to wear shorts on holiday once a year, where nobody knows you and you have power of veto over the photos, but not in front of the neighbours. Not worth the embarrassment. Instead, accept that the only running you want to be involved in is that of a nice hot bath.

'Jogging is for people who aren't intelligent enough to watch breakfast television.'

VICTORIA WOOD

———

And now for some quips:

* How can anyone believe in survival of the fittest when you see some of the people running around in jogging shorts?

* Running is wonderful. Many of us could sit and watch it all day.

* Mindfulness says that a sweet life is a sweaty life. Who knew that there were so many sweet people travelling on the London Underground in rush hour?

* A wife looked disdainfully at her overweight husband and said: 'You should jog around the block.' He replied: 'Why?' 'I'm already here.'

* Remember, the second most important thing after choosing the right running shoe is choosing the left one.

* Fun run: one of life's great oxymorons.

'I go running when I have to; when the ice cream van is doing sixty.'

WENDY LIEBMAN

'I'm on a strict running programme. I started yesterday. I've only missed one day so far.'

KEVIN NEALON

An overweight man went to the doctor who advised him to lose three stone. The doctor recommended that the man should run five miles every day for the next hundred days. The patient phoned the doctor exactly a hundred days later.

'Have you lost the weight?' asked the doctor.

'I have,' said the patient, 'but I'm not at all happy with the situation.'

'Why not?'

'Because I'm five hundred miles from home.'

A middle-aged jogger met his friend in the street. 'I didn't know you'd started running,' said the friend. 'You never struck me as the keep-fit type.'

'I wasn't,' said the jogger, 'but my doctor told me that if I took up jogging, it could add ten years to my life. And he was right. I now feel ten years older.'

Q: How do you know when somebody has run a marathon?

A: Don't worry, they'll tell you.

GRUMPY OLD WALKING

An early morning walk is good for you, because it means your day can only get better. And it is an accepted fact that a walk in the country can only be undertaken when there is a pub at the end of it. However, one of the problems with country walks is that reaching your destination is often easier said than done.

It all starts out promisingly enough with a clear signpost at the head of a visible footpath, but before long, signposts have an unfortunate habit of vanishing altogether while the path becomes markedly less distinct, with chest-high vegetation prompting a suspicion that you are entering leopard territory. Even without any kind of map, you remain quietly confident in your sense of direction, but after ploughing through cow pats and a field patrolled by a marauding bull, and realizing that the tree you have just passed was the same one you saw forty-five minutes earlier, you decide to swallow your pride and ask a passer-by for directions to the Rose and Crown.

The chances are that the first person you ask will say, 'Sorry don't live round 'ere'. The second will be a true local – 'To the Rose and Crown? In them shoes!'

– before issuing directions tailored to local knowledge. 'Right, now you carry straight on to Mary's farm, then take a left at the hawthorn hedge, bear round to the right past Old Dyke Pond, cross over past the cottage where my Uncle Bernard used to live, turn left before you get to the corn field, keep to the right of the Old Brook, do a left at the sweet chestnut tree, carry on down there for three miles and you can't miss it.'

By then, of course, you have completely lost the will to live and your mind has simply glazed over. You can hear the words but you're not taking them in, rather like the time when you were forced to engage in small talk with a scaffolding enthusiast at a party. Obviously asking the local to repeat the directions is not an option, so you bid him a cheery farewell, thank him for his time and set off in search of somebody more coherent.

Apparently, if you are taking a mindful city walk, you are doing more than simply getting from A to B. You are observing *everything* around you – which all too often means discarded burger wrappers, squished dog's mess on the pavement, kamikaze cyclists, pedestrians who don't look where they are going because they are glued to their phone, market researchers poised with clipboards, old boy racers on their mobility scooters and the fact that, despite that morning's weather forecast 100 per cent promising a dry day, it's clearly about to rain.

You can wear fitness trackers that record the number of steps you take each day. Alarmingly, these gadgets will remind you if you are failing to meet your target, which means you might need to end the day by hiking up and down stairs a thousand times. This is nothing new. Many of us have been doing it for years: it's called forgetting what you went upstairs for.

————

'I like long walks, especially when they are taken by people who annoy me.'

FRED ALLEN

————

The only exercise that comes naturally to grumpy old gits is rambling, because once they start a story they can go on for ages. And talking of rambling ...

A group of friends went off rambling one day and paired off in the afternoon before meeting up again in the local pub in the evening. That evening one of the party, Alec, walked into the bar alone with a heavy rucksack on his back.

'Hey, Alec, where's Norman?' asked the other ramblers.

'He must have had a heart attack,' said Alec. 'He just keeled over suddenly and died on the path a couple of miles up the hill.'

The others were horrified. 'Do you mean to say you just left him there but carried the rucksack back here?'

'It was a difficult decision to make,' admitted Alec, 'but I figured that Norman wouldn't get stolen.'

A cautionary tale regarding the potential pitfalls of walking occurred in County Durham in 2009. While out for a walk near Barnard Castle, sixty-six-year-old George Stastny tripped on a narrow footpath and fell down a twenty-foot cliff. Luckily his fall was broken by rocks and trees, and his wife Mary managed to drag him back to the top before hurrying off to fetch help. No sooner had she turned to leave than her husband stood up, fainted, and fell back down the same cliff, landing in the same place. He said afterwards that he thought to himself: 'I've seen this branch before.' Mrs Stastny added: 'I keep telling George that to fall off a cliff once is unfortunate, to fall off a cliff twice is just ridiculous.'

GRUMPY OLD YOGA

Take up yoga if you must – but remember to keep paramedics on speed dial in case you need help getting back up. Anyway, always bear in mind:

* You know you need to exercise more when your pants say yoga but your stomach says Burger King.

* 'I forgot to go to yoga yesterday. That makes seven hundred and eighty weeks in a row.'

* Do you remember when yoga was called Twister?

* The only yoga position worth practising regularly is sleeping.

* Yoga is great. You can close your eyes and imagine yourself in a nice, relaxing place – like on your sofa in front of the TV, not doing yoga.

'I tried yoga but found it a bit of a stretch.'

TIM VINE

Two friends of a certain age were discussing their health issues. 'I'm getting seriously worried about my flabby belly,' said one. 'My body is more beached whale than beach ready. I'm thinking about taking up yoga.'

'Yoga?' scoffed the other. 'You must be joking. I've downloaded an app for my phone to stop me even having to stretch for the TV remote!'

A man went to his local gym to ask about yoga classes for beginners. The instructor asked: 'How flexible are you?'

'Well,' said the man, 'I can't do Tuesdays.'

———

Q: Did you hear about the man who had an affair with his yoga teacher?
A: It put them both in a difficult position.

GRUMPY OLD GARDENING

Gardening is another suggested way of exercising, and for most amateur gardeners it does indeed count as a rigorous physical activity. You've got to:

* Dig up plants that have died

* Mow the lawn or, as most of us prefer to describe it, dandelion beheading

* Run outside to shoo birds that are collecting your hanging basket lining for their nest.

* Bend down to pick out the tufts of grass that insist on growing everywhere except in your lawn.

* Stretch up to pick the solitary apple on your tree.

* Drop-kick snails into next door's garden.

* Rush out to rescue the garden chairs that are about to be blown away by a force ten gale.

* Prune. You may scoff at this but extreme pruning not only burns off the calories, it can also be a most effective way of ensuring that a flowering shrub fails to bloom that year.

> *A keen Russian gardener announced his intention to sue a Moscow seed firm after he was knocked unconscious by a 40lb pumpkin. Nikolay Salakhov bought a small packet of pumpkin seeds with the intention of growing them on the terrace of his country home. The description on the seed packet promised that the pumpkins would be no bigger than a pear, but his reached epic proportions and, when he slammed a door behind him, the vibration caused one of the pumpkins to fall and land on his head, leaving him with concussion.*

And now for some handy definitions and tips aplenty:

* Bulb: potential flower buried in autumn, never to be seen again.

* Before starting your lawn mower, always count your toes and choose the ones you'd most like to keep.

* There's a new chemical spray that kills the greenfly on rose bushes. Actually it kills the roses and the greenfly starve to death.

* Gardens need a lot of water – mostly sweat.

* God made rainy days so gardeners could get the housework done.

* The grass may be greener on the other side of the fence, but you can be sure his water bill is higher.

* Every man reaps what he sows in this life – except the average gardener.

———

'To turn ordinary clothes into gardening clothes, simply mix with compost.'

GUY BROWNING

———

'A garden plant is something that dies if you don't water it and rots if you do.'

HENRY BEARD

———

* A garden is never so good as it will be next year.

* If you must garden, don't aim too high. Tailor your ambitions to the practicalities of your own

patch. Remember, none of the great gardens of the world have a washing line running down the middle.

———————

'Perennials are the ones that grow like weeds, biennials are the ones that die this year instead of next, and hardy annuals are the ones that never come up at all.'

KATHARINE WHITEHORN

Before sending her husband shopping, a wife was very insistent that he should only buy organic vegetables. 'If you come home with non-organic, I'll make you take them back,' she warned.

The husband decided to buy the vegetables from a market stall famed for its organic produce but, with his wife's words still ringing in his ears, he was taking no chances. Picking up a lettuce, he asked the stallholder: 'This lettuce is for my wife. Has it been sprayed with any poisonous chemicals?'

'No,' answered the stallholder. 'You'll have to do that yourself.'

Even an experienced gardener can have problems distinguishing between weeds and garden plants. The best way to tell them apart is that if something comes back year after year, looks healthy and is growing vigorously, it's a weed.

———

A wife answered the doorbell. It was their next-door neighbour. 'Can I borrow your lawnmower?'

'No, sorry,' she said. 'He's not home yet.'

Francis Karnes, of Sacramento, California, was charged with reckless endangerment after he pulled a gun and shot his lawnmower when it refused to start.

THE GARDENING YEAR

January

An excellent month for looking out of the window, promising your partner that you're going to do a lot more in the garden this year, and then sitting back down in front of the fire to watch the football.

February

This is the time when all the garden catalogues fall through your letter box, tempting you with beautiful colour photographs of how your plants would look if a combination of your ineptitude and next door's cat didn't manage to kill them off every year. While doing a spot of tidying, you accidentally tread on most of the sprouting bulb shoots that you planted in autumn. Sow sweet pea seeds.

March

Time for that first mow of the lawn, and the realization that your grass to moss ratio is a personal best of 1:20. When pruning roses, remember that rose thorns are designed to scratch you where it hurts most and to latch themselves onto your clothing so that you are trapped like a pike on a fishing hook. You may need to summon a neighbour or

a curious passer-by to extricate you. Sow more sweet pea seeds to replace the first lot that failed to appear.

April

Your garden is invaded by an army of ravenous slugs, hell bent on destruction. Console yourself in the knowledge that if salt is bad for you, it is even worse for slugs. Post pictures online of their bodies bursting open from a surfeit of sodium chloride as a warning to other gastropods in the area. You realize that your faithful garden shears are now so blunt that it would be quicker to trim the edges of your lawn with a pair of nail clippers.

May

With all the buttercups and daisies present, you suspect that if there were a Lawn in Bloom contest you'd win it easily. The only other flower in the garden is a solitary daffodil that somehow survived your February tidy-up. Sow more sweet pea seeds to replace the ones sown in March that were growing nicely until they were eaten by pigeons.

June

Fetch the garden table and chairs out of the garage so that you can relax and enjoy those long, hot summer days. Put the garden table and chairs back in the garage when it rains solidly for three weeks. Take time to listen to the birdsong and the magical sound of a snail's shell being crushed beneath your foot.

July

You put beer traps down to bait slugs and snails, only to find that, like humans, they eat even more when they're drunk. The sweet peas are all about to burst into flower. You can hardly wait for their heavenly scent to fill the air. Enjoy two weeks on holiday away from gardening chores.

August

Return from holiday to find three drunken snails taunting you on the drive. In your absence, modest-sized plants have become veritable triffids and the garden has reverted to wilderness, resulting in three weeks' hard labour to compensate for two weeks away. Dig up and discard the sweet peas that perished while you were on holiday because you forgot to ask your neighbour to water them.

September

Pick a rose for your partner and watch lovingly as she sniffs it. Tenderly wipe the greenfly from the tip of her nose. You find the perfect place to put the garden gnome that friends brought back as a gift from their holiday in Devon – the builder's skip next door.

October

Time to marvel at how whenever it's a windy day every item of litter from miles around somehow ends up on your front garden. Instead of having nothing to look out at, suddenly there are empty crisp packets, Coca-Cola cans, cardboard boxes and used tissues to brighten up the vista. Vow never to try and grow sweet peas again.

November

Your brother-in-law tells you how wonderful his garden has been this year and insists on posting the pictures on his Facebook page to prove it. He tells you he has green fingers. You suspect it's because he picks his nose.

December

The soil in your containers already resembles a slab of Emmental cheese from where the local squirrels have been burying their nuts, reaffirming your view that they're just a bushy tail away from being Grade One vermin. You sit back dreamily and think about the garden, fantasising about how the whole thing would look covered in tarmac. Ultimately, the best way to enjoy gardening is to put on some old clothes, fetch your trusty garden spade from the shed, take a cold beer out of the fridge and tell someone else where to dig.

———

GRUMPY OLD SEX

Another area for potential exercise is, of course, the bedroom. If the most active thing you've ever done in the bedroom is paint the skirting board, now could be the time to broaden your horizons with more energetic sex.

First, let's qualify what is meant by 'more energetic sex'. Since you're no longer in the first flush of youth, avoid anything so vigorous that it makes your nose bleed, but at least try to work up a bit of enthusiasm. At the end you should feel as exhausted as if you'd just been running for the bus rather than simply hanging up your hat.

As you would expect with senior sex there are a number of grey areas, but for grumpy old gits in general, sex presents something of a conundrum. On the one hand, we moan if we're not getting enough of it; on the other, we moan if we have to make too much effort – like first having to inflate the love doll. Even for those with a human partner, extensive and imaginative foreplay is rarely a high priority, often amounting to little more than 'Are you ready yet?' or 'Don't forget to brush your teeth.' So try to love your partner as a sensuous being, not as someone who has spent the morning cleaning the oven. If that proves beyond your capabilities, follow these six steps to make sex less of a chore:

* Never agree to have sex if it clashes with an important game on TV. You could put your back out from twisting to see the screen.

* Set the alarm on your bedside table so that it doesn't drag on for too long.

* Communicate with your partner in bed, even if it's just to say: 'I *think* I switched the gas cooker off.'

* If you think you might get bored, take a book to bed and read it over your partner's shoulder during sex. Or compile your shopping list. You'd be surprised how quickly 'Do we need more fungal nail infection cream?' can kill any moment of passion.

* If you're getting really bored, feign cramp.

* If the doorbell rings just as your partner is on the brink of orgasm, don't ignore it. It could be that parcel you've been waiting for.

———

'As I've got older, I've found that sex from behind has been a godsend. Because with sex from behind, you don't have to look interested.'

FRANK SKINNER

Two old gits were talking about sex. One said: 'I can't remember the last time I got lucky. It's been years since I had sex. What about you?'

His friend replied: 'Actually, I've still got what it takes to get a woman into the bedroom.'

'Oh yes. What's that?'

'A stairlift.'

If after all this, you absolutely insist on increasing the amount of exercise you take, this routine is designed specifically for seniors to build up muscle strength in the arms and shoulders. You should do it three times a week.

Pick up two 5 lb potato sacks and, holding one in each hand, extend your arms out straight from your sides and keep them there for as long as you can. Begin with a minute and then relax. Each day, you will find that you are able to hold the position for a little longer. After a couple of weeks, move up to 10 lb potato sacks, then 50 lb potato sacks and eventually you will feel confident enough to hold a 100 lb potato sack in each hand with your arms out straight for more than a minute. Once you have mastered that level, but only when you are absolutely sure that it will not be placing too great a strain on your body, put a potato in each of the sacks.

A woman from Galati, Romania, spent two days in hospital in 2007 after accidentally swallowing her lover's false teeth during a moment of passion. She told doctors that she had been trying out a 'special type of passionate kiss' with her gentleman friend.

Three old men were discussing their lives.
The first said: 'I'm still a once-a-night man.'
The second said: 'I'm a twice-a-night man.'
The third said: 'My wife will tell you that I'm a five-times-a-night man. You know, I really shouldn't drink so much tea before I go to bed.'

———

My husband complained to me. He said, 'I can't remember when we last had sex.'
And I said, 'Well I can, and that's why we ain't doin' it.'

ROSEANNE BARR

———

Two old friends were chatting in the bar when one suddenly produced a copy of *Penthouse*.

'I'm sorry,' said the other, 'but I don't buy that type of magazine anymore.'

'I didn't know you'd become prudish.'

'I haven't, but with my bad back I can no longer reach the top shelf.'

A couple were sitting quietly on the porch in their rocking chairs when, without warning, the man reached over and prodded his wife in the ribs.

'What was that for?' she demanded.

'That's for forty years of lousy sex!' he replied.

She said nothing, but a few minutes later she slapped him around the face.

'What was that for?' he asked in a state of shock.

'That,' she said, 'is for knowing the difference!'

'The great thing about going to bed with an older man is that at least he vaguely knows what he's doing, especially since the cataract op. And, afterwards, he can bleed the radiators.'

JENNY ÉCLAIR

Sex in your seventies is great, even though with each passing year it becomes harder to see who you're having it with.

———

Safe sex for grumpy old gits means not falling out of bed.

———

Some grumpy old gits indulge in threesomes in case one of them dies halfway through.

Don't forget, your brain needs exercise, too. So spend plenty of time thinking up excuses for not working out.

———

You can always get exercise by acting as a pallbearer for a friend who exercised.

Romanian pensioner Constantin Luican found that calling a chat line can be an expensive business. Far from being stimulated by the sultry tones of the telephone temptress, Luican fell asleep during the call and ran up a bill of fourteen hundred dollars. He refused to pay because he said the line was boring.

3

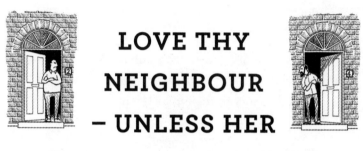

LOVE THY NEIGHBOUR – UNLESS HER HUSBAND'S AT HOME

It is said that in order to experience true inner peace, we must connect with people around us, demonstrate compassion and treat others the way we wish to be treated ourselves. (Note: this may not be advisable if your secret fantasy is for your naked body to be smeared with honey while you are tied to railroad tracks.) Alternatively, we must simply hope that some people will continue to love us in spite of our grumpiness.

As you journey through life, take a moment every now and then to think about others ...

* Because there's every chance they could be plotting something.

* If you want others to be happy, practise compassion; if you want others to be unhappy, practise the cello.

* And why make one person unhappy when, with a little more thought and effort, you could spread misery to the entire family?

THE SEVEN RULES FOR A GOOD RELATIONSHIP

1. Try and do a good deed at least once a week: lift your legs out of the way while your partner is vacuuming near the sofa.

2. Appreciate the amount of effort your partner puts in to make the relationship work. Just

because you take out the trash once, don't make it sound like you've cleaned the whole house.

3. Never ignore your partner when she has something she wants to get off her chest. At least pretend to be listening.

4. Why be difficult when you can go the extra mile and be downright impossible?

5. Everyone is entitled to their point of view; it's not your fault that yours is always the right one.

6. The secret to enjoying someone's company is not to spend a lot of time with them.

7. Try being a cloud to someone's rainbow.

'My wife always complains that I never listen to her – or something like that.'

STEWART FRANCIS

A husband and wife were chatting with friends when the subject of marriage counselling came up. The husband said: 'Oh, we'll never need that. My wife and I have a great relationship. She has a communications degree and I have a degree in theatre arts. She communicates really well and I just act like I'm listening.'

A wife grew bored with the fact that all her husband wanted to do every night was watch TV. Hour after hour he was glued to the set. So one evening she turned to him and asked: 'Do you think the excitement and romance has gone from our marriage?' He snapped: 'I'll discuss it with you during the next commercial break.'

It's also essential to remember that:

* Laughter isn't always the best medicine. If you're really sick, you should ring the emergency services.

* Laugh and the world laughs with you, snore and you sleep alone.

* If a smile can open many doors, why do the police find a battering ram more effective?

* Happiness is not when a clown performs his circus routine with a bucket of water: happiness is when he stops.

* If you think there is good in everyone, you haven't met everyone.

A grumpy old git decided to do something nice for a change. He told his wife: 'I'm going to make you the happiest woman in the world.' She looked at him with surprising tenderness and replied: 'I'll miss you.'

———

'Always smile first thing in the morning.
Might as well get it over with.'

W.C. FIELDS

A couple's relationship was going through a rocky phase where all lines of communication had broken down. They had not spoken to each other for days. At the height of the acrimony, the husband realized that he needed his wife to wake him at 5 am so that he could catch an early morning business flight. Not wanting to be the first to break the silence, he wrote on a piece of paper: Please wake me at 5 am.

The next morning, he woke to discover to his horror that it was half-past eight and that he had missed his flight. He was about to berate his wife when he noticed a slip of paper on his pillow. It read: *'It is 5 am. Wake up.'*

RANDOM ACTS OF GRUMPINESS

A flash of grumpiness will make someone's day truly unforgettable. In the unlikely event that you may be running out of things to be grumpy about, follow a few of these Top 6 suggestions:

1. Start the day by complaining bitterly that the birdsong woke you up too early. You don't want to hear chirpiness at that time of the morning, or at any time of the day. It goes against the grain.

2. Moan about the toaster's constant – some might say wilful – refusal to brown both sides of the bread evenly. And who put the knife that had been used for marmalade back in the butter dish?

3. Berate the postman for being even later than usual. Tell him you can remember the time when the morning mail was exactly that, delivered in the morning, not at 2.30 pm. Remind him that you live in the middle of a city, not on some remote island off the coast of Scotland and watch as he bids you a cheery good-day while scratching his chin with an extended middle finger.

4. Mutter darkly that you keep finding ants in the downstairs toilet. You manage to stamp on one, only to discover that dozens more then turn up for the funeral.

5. Witter on about the quality of modern TV: one hundred and eighty-four channels and nothing to watch. You end up watching the same episode of the same American crime drama that you watched on a different channel earlier in the week.

6. Time for bed, and you discover that your partner, who went up earlier to get away from you, has left you with barely a third of the duvet. It's a good job you're not one to complain.

A man told his friend: 'My wife left me last week. She said I was cold, selfish and uncaring. She said she was going out for some milk and never came back.'

'How are you coping?' asked the friend.

'Oh, not too bad. I've been using some of that powdered stuff.'

And talking about enemies:

* It is far easier to forgive an enemy after you've got even with him.

* Stare at people you don't like through the prongs of a fork and pretend they're in jail.

* Forgive and forget, but keep a list of names just in case.

* Sometimes the first step to forgiveness is coming to the realization that the other person is a total idiot.

* Your enemy may not be the worst person in the world, but until a worse one comes along, he'll do.

* Life would be easier if you could mark people as spam.

'Always forgive your enemies – nothing annoys them so much.'

OSCAR WILDE

When his heavily pregnant wife began to have contractions, Steve Phillips wasted no time in driving her to hospital in Wolverhampton. However, on the way he noticed a fishing tackle shop and thought it would be the perfect opportunity to make a quick stop to get his rod repaired. Leaving his wife outside in the car, it was twenty minutes before he returned . . . with a jar of maggots. Mrs Phillips, who had been in considerable discomfort during his lengthy absence, was furious and said later: 'He put the maggots before our baby!' Her husband explained: 'I knew that we would be busy after the birth and I needed the rod fixed first. The maggots were just an afterthought.'

———

Furious after a row with her husband, a German woman decided to smash up his Ford Fiesta, but after causing thirteen hundred dollars' worth of damage, she realized that she had attacked her neighbour's car by mistake.

FOR WHEN YOU NEED AN EXTRA SPLASH OF THE GRUMPS

* The easiest time to add insult to injury is when you're signing someone's plaster cast.

* Sometimes the best helping hand you can give is a good, firm push.

* Don't kick a man when he's down unless you're absolutely certain he won't get back up.

* And petty jealousy is a waste of emotion. Revenge works much better.

An elderly woman shopper at a supermarket checkout was fumbling in her handbag for her purse when the cashier noticed a TV remote control in there. 'Do you always carry your TV remote in your handbag?' he asked.

'No,' said the woman, 'but my husband refused to come shopping with me, and I reckoned this was the most evil thing I could do to him legally.'

A couple had been married for twenty-four years. At first they used to go out together a lot but, as time passed, he became miserly and set in his ways, preferring to save money by staying at home watching TV. Then one evening, out of the blue, he suddenly announced: 'Put your coat on, darling, I'm going to Jeff's Bar.'

'Are you taking me out for a drink?' she asked excitedly.

'Don't be silly,' he said. 'I'm turning the heating off.'

WHAT IS THE BEST POLICY?

* Honesty is the best policy, but insanity is a better defence.

* Honesty is the best policy, if only because there is less competition.

* Never tell a lie unless it is absolutely convenient.

* Confession is good for your soul, but bad for your career.

* Learn to love yourself, but don't do it in public.

* Love people despite their faults, so long as they don't mention yours.

* Long-distance relationships are like obese people, they rarely work out.

* Take an interest in your partner's life; hire a private detective.

* Some of us learn from the mistakes of others; the rest of us have to be the others.

* Promises are like babies – fun to make but hell to deliver.

*Connect with strangers, even if it's only to tell them to move their car from outside your house.

'Honesty may be the best policy, but it's important to remember that apparently, by elimination, dishonesty is the second-best policy.'

GEORGE CARLIN

A grumpy husband was listing what he perceived as his wife's faults.

'If you learned how to cook and iron,' he grumbled, 'we could do without the maid.'

His wife snapped back: 'And if you learned how to make love, we could do without the gardener.'

―――――――

A husband came home in a foul mood. He said to his wife: 'I hear you've been telling everyone that I'm an idiot!'

'Sorry,' she said, 'I didn't know it was a secret.'

WHO NEEDS FRIENDS?

Making new friends at our age can seem too much like hard work. It's just so exhausting having to be nice to someone all the time. Plus we have to go through our entire life history, warts and all, to a virtual stranger. It's like a trip to a psychiatrist, but without the tea and biscuits.

The only way we can make it work is to operate a one-in, one-out policy; for every new friend, cull an old one. If that sounds brutal, don't fret. The number of crossings-out in our address book each year as we get older means that we can usually rely on the Grim Reaper to make the choice for us.

Jerry was talking in the pub to his only friend in the whole world. He couldn't understand why he was so unpopular.

'Tell me honestly, Jim,' he said, 'why do people take an instant dislike to me?'

'It saves time,' replied Jim.

Convinced that his wife was having an affair, a husband came home to confront her.

'Was it my friend Bill?' he demanded.

'No,' she said.

'Was it my friend Martin?'

'No.'

'Was it my friend Phil?'

'No,' she yelled. 'What is it – don't you think I have any friends of my own?!'

Let's be honest, some friends have their uses:

* Always make friends with recovering alcoholics: that way you're never short of a ride home.

* A lifelong friend is one you haven't borrowed money from yet.

* Everyone should have at least two friends – one to talk to, and one to talk about.

* One good reason for keeping just a small circle of friends is that three out of four murders are committed by people who know the victim.

* A friend in whom you can confide in any circumstance would be a dangerous witness for the prosecution.

Lying on her deathbed, a wife begged her husband: 'You've made most of my life a misery with your constant grumpiness, so at least grant me one final wish to make me happy. After I'm gone, marry my friend Jane.'

'But I thought you hated Jane?' said the husband.

'I do.'

———

'A lot of people say, "A stranger is just a friend you haven't met yet." But I've been mugged four times and I haven't kept in touch with any of them.'

CHRIS STOKES

———

On the other hand:

* A friend in need is a pain in the arse.

* If you help a friend in need, the problem is they will remember you the next time they are in need.

* Never forget a friend, especially if he owes you money.

* Friendship is like incontinence: everyone can see it, but only you can feel its true warmth.

———

'Every time a friend's child succeeds, I feel something so unpleasant there isn't a word for it, not even in German.'

JUDITH WOODS

———————

But can friends be trusted?

* A friend who only sees the good in you is a lousy judge of character.

* A friend is just an enemy who doesn't yet know you very well.

* A friend who is always there for you ought to get a life.

* Friends help you move house. Real friends help you move bodies.

* Friends may come and friends may go, but if you're really unlucky they'll stay for the weekend.

* Never allow your best friends to get lonely. Keep pestering them.

* There are two kinds of friends: those who are around when you need them, and those who are around when they need you.

NEVER, EVER TRUST ...

The following, but you could easily compile your own list:

* A man who carries a small dog.

* A doctor who tries to take your temperature with his finger.

* A surgeon with more than three plasters on his fingers.

* A street vendor who keeps looking over his shoulder.

* Anyone who can save half a Bounty bar for later.

* Anyone who says: 'I'm on your side.'

* A taxi driver who shoots down a side street every time he sees a police car.

* Anyone who says: 'I hear what you say.'

* A stockbroker who is married to a travel agent.

* Anyone with the words 'financial' or 'adviser' in their job title; whose job title runs to more than four words; or anyone who is *always* happy.

Following a restless night, a grumpy old husband sat up in bed, turned to his wife and said: 'I can't believe it! All night long you kept cursing me in your sleep!' She replied drily: 'What made you think I was asleep?'

Never trust a man with testicles.

JO BRAND

The reason why some people have trust issues is because while you can buy two pairs of underpants in an identical size only one of them will fit.

FAMILY FEUDS

The older you get, the more you look at other people and ask yourself: 'Do I really want to be related to them?' Especially ... which reminds me:

* Any of your friends can become an enemy, but a relative is one from the start.

* The best way to get in touch with long-lost relatives is to win the lottery.

* Blood is thicker than water, and much more difficult to get out of the carpet.

* The family that sticks together should bathe more often.

————

'The first half of our lives is ruined by our parents, and the second half by our children.'

CLARENCE DARROW

————

A man took his dog to the vet and asked the vet to cut off its tail.

'Why do you want to do that?' asked the vet.

'Because my sister is coming tomorrow, and I don't want anything to make her think she's welcome.'

————

Short of ideas for what to get her sister's curmudgeonly brother for his birthday, a woman decided that a novel present would be to buy him a large plot in an exclusive cemetery. The following year, however, she didn't buy him anything, which prompted him to complain even more bitterly than usual.

'What are you moaning about?' she said. 'You still haven't used the present I got you last year!'

A grumpy old git answered his front door to find his sister-in-law standing on the step with a suitcase.

'Can I stay here for a few days?' she asked.

'Of course you can,' he said, and shut the door in her face.

———

And yes, train your mind to see the good in absolutely everyone, except for:

* Neighbours whose car alarms go off in the middle of the night.

* Queue jumpers.

* Dog walkers who let their animals decorate the pavement and then don't pick it up.

* Workmen who show up a day later than they promised.

* People who are incapable of shutting car doors quietly.

* Anyone who uses 'less than' when it should be 'fewer than'.

* Anyone who writes 'should of'.

* Anyone who uses the word 'banter' or worse still 'bants'.

* Passengers on public transport who put their feet up on the seat opposite.

* Slow-moving pedestrians who walk down the street four abreast.

* Any company spokesperson who uses the phrase: 'Lessons have been learned.'

* Dental hygienists who think the most important thing going on in your life is a small build-up of plaque.

* News headline writers who put the fear of God into their readers by using daft words like 'snowbomb' to describe what amounts to little more than a light dusting of snow.

* Taxi drivers who take you the longest way from A to B.

* Train passengers who place their bag on the seat next to them, apparently in the belief that it has purchased a ticket.

* Anyone who misuses an apostrophe.

* Anyone who uses the word 'journey' without physically going anywhere.

* Anyone who uses the word 'awesome' to describe something distinctly average.

* Anyone who is younger, more successful and better looking than you.

* But especially tourists who ask you to take a photo of them and their partner, and then hand you a state-of-the-art camera and tripod with a list of operational instructions that would tax David Bailey. They then grumble when you are singularly unable to master either the advanced focusing mechanism or the latest P25XXX shutter speed function and end up chopping their heads off in the photo.

———

Despairing at their lack of a social life, a wife turned to her husband and said: 'Let's go out and have some fun tonight.'

'Okay,' he said, 'but if you get home before I do, leave the hall light on.'

A Russian man divorced his wife of eighteen years after discovering that she had been making him eat cheap pumpkins instead of courgettes. As soon as he found pumpkin rind in the garbage bin, Ivan Dimitrov realized the truth about the pies his wife Irena had been feeding him for the last six months and instigated divorce proceedings. He said: 'She knows I absolutely hate pumpkins and she lied to me for months about it just because the pumpkins were cheap. What else has she been lying about? What man could trust a woman who fed him pumpkins for half a year?'

4

OLD DOG, NEW TRICKS?
NO THANKS

One of the most popular New Year's resolutions is to take up a new hobby, something that will stop you taking root on the sofa. But if you're one of those people who only ever walked the path less travelled because you were lost, starting a new challenge can be a daunting prospect. Not least because it requires some effort, and most of your energy is expended on the all too regular battles you face with the likes of customer care phone numbers that keep bleating 'your call is important to us' (if it's that important, *answer the damn phone*) and hotels which fail to explain that the promised 'partial sea view' from your room is only attainable by hanging out of the window, turning your head at ninety degrees and using a telescope.

But let's get down to detail. Being grumpy is an art, so keep practising:

* Don't allow your life (or wife) to stagnate as you get older. Every day, try to find something new to complain about.

* Don't try anything that you're not prepared to explain to a paramedic.

* Broaden your horizons by collecting things, even though the only thing you have collected so far in life is dust.

* And don't forget that (1) variety may be the spice of life, but monotony pays for the groceries and (2) nothing dispels enthusiasm like a small admission fee.

Why do people who want to bully you into trying new things try to justify it by saying, 'Life is short'? What does that mean? Life is the longest thing anyone ever does. Are they going to do something that's longer?

GRUMPY OLD GOLF

If there is one pursuit guaranteed to bring out the grumpy side of even the most mild-mannered individual, it is golf. It is, as Winston Churchill famously said, 'a game whose aim is to hit a very small ball into an even smaller hole with weapons singularly ill-designed for the purpose.' No wonder that golf brings out the worst aspects of human nature.

Cheating at golf is an art form in itself as participants suddenly lose the ability to count beyond five and a ball that was last seen heading into such dense woodland that Tarzan might feel at home there, miraculously reappears – via the player's pocket – in a good position with a clear shot to the green. So if you are prone to being grumpy already (and you probably are if you're reading this book) golf will provide you with a whole new raft of opportunities for temper tantrums and fits of pique. If, on

the other hand, you are searching for serenity, give it a miss, just like the ball.

So what do we know about golf? Well, apart from the fact that it involves a ridiculous amount of walking, broken up by disappointment and bad arithmetic and that it's a game invented by people who think music comes out of a bagpipe, it has the following points to recommend it:

* Once the sport of the wealthy and the privileged, today it is open to anyone who owns ridiculous clothes.

* No matter how badly you play, it is always possible to get worse.

* If the ball goes right, it's a slice; if it goes left, it's a hook; and if it goes straight, it's a miracle.

* Some wives have the wrong idea about golf – they think their husbands are out enjoying themselves.

* A ball you can see in the rough from fifty yards away is not yours.

* After six months of lessons, you find that you have a great short game – but unfortunately it's off the tee.

* If your opponent has difficulty remembering whether he shot a six or a seven, he probably shot an eight.

* Golf scores are directly proportional to the number of witnesses.

* It's amazing how a golfer who never helps around the house will replace his divots, repair his ball marks and rake a bunker.

* The shortest distance between any two points on a golf course is a straight line that passes directly through the centre of a very large tree.

A golfer was lining up his drive when a voice from the clubhouse called out: 'Will the gentleman on the ladies' tee please move back to the men's tee!'

The golfer ignored the request and continued with his practice swings. The voice called out again: 'Sir, will you please move back to the men's tee *now*!'

The golfer carried on regardless and was just addressing the ball when the voice called out for a third time: 'You are violating club rules! Move back to the men's tee *immediately* or I will have you thrown off the course!'

The golfer turned angrily in the direction of the clubhouse and shouted back: 'Do you mind shutting up while I play my second shot!'

'They call it golf because all the other four-letter words were taken.'

RAYMOND FLOYD

Golf enables you to scale new heights of frustration as you discover that your divots go further than your drives, and that the only round in which you ever hit two good balls is when you accidentally stand on the bunker rake.

When two friends met in the bar, the conversation turned to golf.

'I had my first lesson last week,' said one.

'How did you get on?' asked the other.

'It went really well. After just one lesson I could throw my clubs as far as guys who have been playing for years.'

———

New golfer: 'I can't get the hang of this game. Where am I going wrong?'

Coach: 'Your problem is you're standing too close to the ball – after you've hit it.'

'The reason the pro tells you to keep your head down is so you can't see him laughing.'

PHYLLIS DILLER

––––––––

If you take up golf in your seventies, you always hope to be able to shoot your age, but you're more likely to shoot your weight instead.

––––––––

When you look up and cause a terrible shot, you can guarantee that you will look down again at exactly the moment when you should be watching the ball if you want to have any hope of ever seeing it again.

––––––––

How do you know when your golf game is improving? You're missing the ball by much less than you used to.

Halfway through his backswing while driving off at the seventeenth hole at Lyme Regis Golf Club, Dorset, sixty-nine-year-old Derek Gatley received a painful blow when the steel shaft of his club snapped, hit him on the back of the head and knocked him out. When he came round, Mr Gatley admitted: 'It was the first thing I had hit all day.'

A man and a woman were standing at the altar about to get married when the bride-to-be spotted that the prospective groom had a set of golf clubs with him.

'What on earth are you doing with those golf clubs in church?' she hissed.

'Well,' he said, 'this isn't going to take all afternoon, is it?'

―――――

A heavily overweight man had tried all kinds of exercise to slim down – swimming, running, aerobics – but nothing seemed to work. As a last resort his doctor suggested that he take up golf, adding: 'There's no finer game.'

So the man went out and bought a set of golf clubs but a few weeks later he returned to the doctor to ask if he could take up a different sport.

'Why? What was the problem with golf?' asked the doctor.

'Well,' explained the man, indicating his sizeable girth, 'the trouble is that when I put the ball where I can see it, I can't reach to hit it. And when I put it where I can hit it, I can't see it!'

Playing in a qualifying round of the 1912 Shawnee Invitational for Ladies tournament at Shawnee-on-Delaware, Pennsylvania, US golfer Maud McInnes took 166 strokes for the 133 yard, par three, sixteenth hole. Her problems began when she drove her tee shot into the fast-flowing Binniekill River and the ball sailed off downstream. Instead of taking a penalty and hitting another tee shot, the resourceful Maud clambered into a rowing boat with her husband at the oars and set off in pursuit of her ball. A mile and a half further down the river, while her faithful spouse kept score, she finally succeeded on beaching the ball on terra firma. She then had to hack her way through woodland and dense undergrowth to make it back to the sixteenth green. And so it was that 165 shots and nearly two hours after teeing off, she holed out. It is not known whether she qualified for the later stages of the tournament.

GRUMPY OLD FISHING

To millions of people across the world, fishing is the ultimate combination of fresh air and relaxation, of being at one with nature. To others, it appears a pointless exercise, nothing more than man's attempt to outwit a fish, a sector of wildlife that has barely evolved for millions of years. And if you do manage to catch something other than a plastic bag or a shopping cart, you invariably have to throw it back so that someone else will have the chance to catch it. So you're not really owning that fish, you're just renting it for a photo opportunity.

Then, of course, there are the ones that got away, which is why the collective noun for a group of anglers is called an exaggeration. Only an angler could make a stickleback sound like Jaws. In fact, the only time a fisherman tells the truth is when he calls another fisherman a liar. But, as with every hobby, there are good and bad things about fishing.

'There's a fine line between fishing and just standing on the shore like an idiot.'

STEVEN WRIGHT

————

Fishing – the good points:

* You get to sit down all day, often with beer.

And the bad:

* You get to sit down all day, on an uncomfortable seat and on a muddy riverbank in pouring rain.

* You have to get up ridiculously early in the morning.

* The only thing a novice angler is ever likely to catch is a cold.

* The only bite you'll get is from mosquitoes.

* The only people you get to talk to all day are other anglers.

* Oh, and one more good thing. After spending a day fishing, nothing else in life will ever seem quite as boring again.

————

A boy burst into the house in floods of tears after spending a day fishing with his father. His mother asked him what was wrong.

The boy explained: 'Dad and I were fishing and he hooked this giant fish, the biggest he'd ever seen. But while he was reeling it in, the line broke and the fish got away.'

'Come on, Billy,' she said, 'a big boy like you shouldn't be crying about an accident. You should have just laughed it off.'

'But that's exactly what I did, Mum.'

The 1972 UK National Ambulance Servicemen's Angling Championships, staged at Kidderminster, proved something of a disappointment. After spending five hours on a canal side, the two hundred paramedics had not managed to catch a single fish. It was only then that a passer-by casually informed them that all the fish had been moved to another location three weeks earlier.

GRUMPY OLD DANCING

We grumpy old gits are no strangers to treading on people's toes from time to time, which means that taking up ballroom dancing is not a particularly good idea. Inspired by TV shows like *Strictly Come Dancing* or *Dancing with the Stars*, your partner may suggest that you learn the foxtrot, waltz or tango. 'It will be something we can do together,' they'll say. If doing something together is the guiding factor, what's wrong with eating or sleeping? You'd even be prepared to change your nightly routine so that the two of you flossed your teeth together in front of the bathroom mirror. At least you won't have to dress up in tight, thrombosis-inducing pants and a pink ruffled shirt to do it.

————

'I could dance with you until the cows come home. On second thoughts, I'd rather dance with the cows until you come home.'

GROUCHO MARX, *DUCK SOUP*

————

There are many other forms of dancing, all of which should be similarly avoided if you wish to safeguard both your shins and your dignity. Salsa dancing is suspiciously like keeping fit (see Chapter 2), line dancing is fine if you're happy being compared to Hoss Cartwright from TV's *Bonanza*, while energetic dad-dancing may look as if you have just been zapped with an electric cattle prod. And don't forget: dancing is the art of pulling your feet away faster than your partner can step on them.

GRUMPY OLD ORNITHOLOGY

Bird watching always seems like a lot of effort for something that can be experienced far better by staying at home and watching TV. Why trudge out for miles in all weathers to woodlands and wetlands for a possible fleeting glimpse of some unusual bird when TV nature programmes provide you with perfect views every time, without having to move from the sofa? If you really want to see a bird at close quarters, try eating a prawn sandwich on a seafront bench when seagulls are around.

Encouraging birds into your own garden is a different matter, however, and the best way to do that is either to sow grass seed or to wash your car.

The other problem is professional bird-watchers, or twitchers as they are known. These are the extreme wing of ornithology, die-hards who would cheerfully trample you underfoot in their rush to catch sight of a Siberian thrush or an Eastern crowned warbler. Once the word is out that a rare bird has been spotted, twitchers flock in their hundreds to the location, binoculars at the ready. They are more determined than the paparazzi in pursuit of a fallen celebrity. Nothing is allowed to get in the way of a twitcher, so if you ever see an extremely rare bird in your garden, zip it.

GRUMPY OLD LEARNING A FOREIGN LANGUAGE

If you have too much time on your hands, you are sometimes encouraged to expand your skill set by learning a new language. It will be another string to your bow, you are told. But your habit of shouting at foreigners loudly and slowly in English, coupled with the international language of mime, has enabled you to converse perfectly adequately with them for years. If, however, you do get talked into learning a foreign language, here are some handy French phrases you might care to master:

À quelle heure de la journée appelez-vous cela?
What time of the day do you call this?

Je me souviens quand c'était tous les champs.
I can remember when this was all fields.

Où sont mes clés? Qui a caché mes clés?
Where are my keys? Who's hidden my keys?

Ce pays va ruiner.
This country's going to the dogs.

Qu'est-ce que je dois faire être servi ici?
What do I have to do to get served around here?

Allez vous faire foutre! Je dirai à vos parents ce que vous avez fait.
Clear off! Wait till I tell your parents!

Où est le gérant? Je demande à parler au gérant.
Where's the manager? I demand to speak to the manager.

Vous appelez ça de la musique? Ce n'est rien d'autre qu'un bruit!
You call that music? It's nothing but a noise!

Quand j'avais votre âge …
When I was your age …

GRUMPY OLD TRAVEL

If you've spent the last forty years in and around your home town apart from two weeks every September in a caravan at a coastal resort thirty miles away, the idea of venturing abroad – to *another* country – probably seems inconceivable. You can understand why. There are the passports to pay for, flights to book with so many hidden extras that you can see the cost taking off before your eyes, the three-hour wait at the airport – and that's if you're lucky enough to be travelling on one of the six weeks in the year when the French air traffic controllers aren't on strike. Then, even when you reach your destination, there's the language, the foreign food and probably the heat.

And what do you come home to? A pile of washing and ironing, the summit of which could only be reached with the aid of sherpas, and the realization that the only food in the house is a bruised banana and a box of crunchy cat treats. So why bother? If your partner wants to see the world, buy them an atlas and remind them:

* Travel not only broadens the mind but, especially with French food, it also broadens the waist.

* If you look like your passport photo, you're probably not well enough to travel.

* It is perfectly possible to spend your entire holiday on a winding mountain road behind a large motorhome.

* A staycation is a wonderful opportunity to hear rain lashing down in a different location.

* If you don't want to go abroad on holiday, you can achieve the same effect by staying at home and tipping every second person you see.

––––––––

'There are only two reasons to sit in the back row of an airplane: either you have diarrhoea, or you're anxious to meet people who do.'

RICH JENI

If you have booked your hotel with an online travel company, on your return you will probably receive an email saying: 'Now you're back. Where to next?' Talk about pushing for business! Give me a chance. I haven't unpacked yet! Or they send you details about 'awesome' deals on hotels in the very town where you live. I live there, you muppets! I've got a perfectly good bed here already, so I've no intention of paying for one, no matter how awesome the deal.

A couple from Montreal were talking about their holiday to a friend. 'It sounds like you had a great time in California,' said the friend, 'but I didn't know you were planning to take in Florida as well.'

'We weren't,' said the wife, 'but Ted simply will not ask for directions!'

'There ain't no surer way to find out whether you like people or hate them than to travel with them.'

MARK TWAIN

An elderly American tourist had to be rescued from the depths of a Bavarian forest in 2004 after losing his way while consulting a ninety-year-old guidebook. Seventy-nine-year-old Hank Edwards had longed to visit that part of Germany ever since reading Beautiful Bayreuth, *a guidebook purchased by his father in 1914. But by following the book's directions, he ended up becoming stranded in the Bayreuth forest for two days. The local tourist board pointed out that two World Wars and a massive reforestation programme had changed the region considerably.*

DID I MENTION AIRLINES?

Let flying be an ethereal experience as you glide effortlessly across the sky – even though the child behind you has kicked the back of your seat incessantly since take off, the head of the passenger next to you is leaning on your shoulder because he has fallen asleep with rivulets of drool trickling from the corner of his mouth, and three people have beaten you to the toilet because your path has been blocked by the inconsiderate halfwit on the next row who feels the need to rummage through his bag in the overhead locker every two minutes.

Here are some Don'ts:

* Fly with an airline where the plane has an outside toilet.

* Fly with an airline where, before take-off, the passengers get together and elect a pilot.

* Fly with an airline where there's a resident chaplain on board.

* And never use a train toilet that has an automatic door. If you haven't mastered the locking device, it can slide open when you

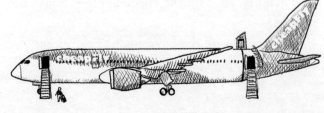

least expect it in full view of other passengers.
You might as well be doing a dump in a shop
window.

And did you know:

* The only good thing about airline food is that
  they're considerate enough to give you small
  portions.

* You don't need a movie on some airlines,
  because your life keeps flashing before your eyes.

* Anyway, if flying is so safe, why do they call the
  airport 'the terminal'?

———

Why do they sell luggage in shops at airports?
Who on earth forgets their suitcase when going on
holiday?

———

A passenger walked up to the airline check-in desk
and announced: 'I want you to send one of my cases
to Stockholm, another to Paris, and the third one to
Rome.'

'I'm sorry, sir,' said the check-in clerk, 'that's not
possible.'

'Why not?' said the passenger. 'That's what you
did to my luggage last year!'

When an airplane encountered some turbulence, it started juddering and rocking from side to side. In an effort to keep the passengers calm, the flight attendant wheeled out the drinks trolley.

'Would you like a drink?' she asked a male passenger in business class.

'Why not?' he said icily. 'I'll have whatever the pilot's been having.'

An irate airline passenger ate his winning scratch card in protest at not being able to claim the money immediately. The man was flying with Ryanair from Krakow in Poland to East Midlands Airport in England in 2010 when he won 10,000 euros with the scratch card. The flight crew confirmed that he had won the prize but told him that because it was such a large sum, he would have to collect the jackpot directly from the company that ran the competition. Ryanair said the man then became frustrated and started to eat his winning ticket, thus making it impossible for him to claim the prize money. A Ryanair spokesman said: 'He clearly felt that we should have had his ten thousand euros kicking around on the aircraft.'

AS FOR CRUISES . . .

* Think twice before boarding a cruise ship where the passengers are supplied with oars.

* A cruise holiday is when you go for days and days . . . and see nothing but food.

* A dream holiday would be one where all your family gets along.

———

'The vast majority of passengers on a cruise liner are there against their will.'

PETER TINNISWOOD

———

. . . AND TRAINS

In theory, it should be the most relaxing form of transport. No shaking your fist at other drivers, nobody waking you up during your journey to tell you about an amazing offer on cheap perfume, and, unless the weather has really taken a turn for the worse, you are almost guaranteed not to be seasick.

Yet the reality is that train travel is far from a stress-free experience. Even if you have booked a seat in advance, there is no certainty that you'll actually get one because all too often reserved seats are not marked. Usually this is because the train staff didn't have time due to a quick turnaround or that old reliable 'technical fault'. So you either have to argue with the stranger sitting in your reserved seat, hope that there is a spare seat somewhere else, which is only empty because the person in the next seat is eating an iffy boiled egg sandwich, or stand in the doorway where you have to move every couple of minutes to allow someone to enter or leave the toilet. And have you risked looking inside?

Then there is always the possibility, particularly if you are travelling on a Bank Holiday or weekend, that your train will not be running at all due to 'essential engineering works'. This, you are informed, is to offer a hugely improved service at some mythical date in the future. But don't worry, the train company will not leave you stranded, which is why in Britain we pride ourselves on having the best replacement bus service in the world.

————

A train was crawling along slowly until finally it creaked to a halt. A passenger saw the guard walking by outside.

'What's the problem?' shouted the passenger, leaning out of the window.

'There's a cow on the track,' replied the guard.

Ten minutes later, the train resumed its slow pace, but within a couple of minutes it had ground to a halt again.

The same passenger saw the guard walking outside once more. 'What happened?' he called out. 'Did we catch up with the cow again?'

Unlike British trains, Japanese rail services are renowned for their punctuality, offering profuse apologies to passengers even if they are a minute late. But passengers on Honshu were delayed for two hours when their train was brought to a halt after running over an army of millipedes. As they were crushed, the insects' body fluids were squashed out, acting as a lubricant and causing the train's wheels to slip on the track.

5

EVERYTHING YOU EAT IS BAD FOR YOU

Never a day passes without a scare story about a certain foodstuff that has suddenly been branded detrimental to our health. All change. Another disruption. More grump. Of course, we should all strive for a sensible, balanced diet but it's not easy any more to know what's good and bad. Last week a square of chocolate was good for your wellbeing, today it is the tool of the devil. But not just chocolate, processed meat too, i.e., sausages and bacon. And think for a moment who has most to gain from pushing out these new negative stories about sausages and bacon. That's right: pigs. George Orwell was right all along.

So what's the first modern, most idiotic piece of newfangled food advice we do NOT need? Right. The diet. As we reach middle age and beyond, we invariably find that our hair thins and our waistline expands. We no longer measure success by the number of notches on our bedpost but by the number of notches we need in order to fasten the belt of our trousers. It is commonly known as 'middle-age spread' and is often the result of eating what we liked in our younger years. We're not talking school dinners here, but the time in our twenties when we feasted to our heart's content on pizzas, burgers and ice cream. Now it's payback time, and suddenly all the foods we once loved are bad for us.

We are told that we have to change our diet, cutting right down on fatty, tasty foods and replacing them with the healthy and bland. We have to eat less of what we like and more of what we don't like. The Spanish Inquisition never devised anything so fiendish. Or we could just carry on regardless, deciding we could easily be hit by a bus tomorrow and that we would probably have a greater chance of surviving the impact if we still had some padding around the middle.

———

THE SEVEN RULES OF DIETING

1. If you eat something when nobody is watching, it has no calories.

2. When drinking a diet cola while eating a chocolate bar, the calories in the chocolate bar are cancelled out by the diet cola.

3. Foods that are the same colour have the same

amount of calories, such as spinach and pistachio ice cream.

4. Food that is licked off knives, spoons or container lids while you are preparing a dish has no calories.

5. Food that is eaten off someone else's plate has no calories.

6. Broken cookies contain no calories, because the act of breaking them causes all the calories to fall out.

7. Food eaten on holidays abroad doesn't count. So don't feel guilty when you tuck into that breakfast of bacon, sausages, fried egg, tomatoes, beans, mushrooms and hash browns. All the calories will be absorbed by the airplane cabin pressure on the flight home.

And remember:

* Food has never made you fat, but scales always do.

* Good health is merely the slowest possible rate at which you can die.

* Live the actual moment – have another chocolate cookie.

* Smoking will kill you, bacon will kill you, but smoking bacon will cure it.

* You could always try the garlic diet. You don't lose any weight, but from the distance they will keep, your friends will think you look slimmer.

* The second day of a diet is always easier than the first. By the second day you're off it. Dieting is a piece of cake.

Q: What's the most fattening thing you can put in a banana split?
A: A spoon.

Mindfulness says you can think yourself thin. Stand in front of the mirror with your belly bulging and repeat over and over: 'I am slim, I am slim.' The psychoanalytical term for this practice is delusion.

'Life expectancy would grow by leaps and bounds if green vegetables smelled as good as bacon.'

DOUG LARSON

———————

A man was standing on the bathroom scales, desperately sucking his stomach in. His wife, thinking he was trying to reduce his weight, commented: 'I don't think that will help.'

'It does,' he said. 'It's the only way I can read the numbers!'

———————

Scientific tests show that eating a square of dark chocolate can lift your spirits and lead to increased happiness, so think how much happier you would be with two squares or even an entire bar.

———————

'I'm sick of listening to otherwise intelligent people moaning about being faint with hunger when they're on some ridiculous, self-inflicted, five-hundred-calorie-a-day diet. Yes, you're hungry; you're also very boring. So shut up about it or open the biscuits.'

JENNY ÉCLAIR

A German man's love of beer proved his undoing after he fell into an open drain – and was unable to get out because of his beer belly. Forty-six-year-old Gerhard Wilder, from Bochum, was wedged so tightly that he had to be freed by firefighters. After embarrassing pictures of his plight appeared in the German media, he vowed to stay off the beer and go on a diet.

'I refuse to spend my life worrying about what I eat. There's no pleasure worth foregoing just for an extra three years in the geriatric ward.'

JOHN MORTIMER

Mindful eating requires you not to rush your food. You must savour every mouthful, taste the moment. But at our age with hot, spicy food there's no time to waste because it can be coming out of the other end before we know it.

A woman at a diet club was lamenting the fact that she had put on weight. 'I made my family's favourite chocolate cake over the weekend,' she told the group, 'and they ate half of it after dinner. The next day, I kept staring at the other half until my resolve finally weakened and I cut myself a thin slice.

'Well, I'm ashamed to say that once I got the taste for it there was no stopping me. One slice led to another and soon the whole cake was gone. I was totally dismayed by my lack of willpower, and I knew that my husband would be bitterly disappointed in me.'

'What did he say when he found out?' asked the group leader sympathetically.

'Oh, he never found out,' said the woman. 'I just made another cake and ate half!'

So, what do we know? Well, dieticians and nutritionists keep trying to persuade us to try new foods that are supposed to be beneficial to our health. All this really means is that scientists have not yet got round to discovering the downsides. Remember when smoking was meant to be good for your wellbeing? That's not a line they roll out too often these days. But while tempting you with weird new foods, health experts sometimes quietly

acknowledge that 'they may be an acquired taste'. Sorry, chum, but anything for which you need an acquired taste is not meant to be eaten.

A man in his fifties was seriously overweight, so his doctor put him on a diet. 'I want you to eat regularly for two days, then skip a day, and repeat the process for two weeks. The next time I see you, you should have lost at least five pounds.'

But when the man returned two weeks later, he had lost 20 lb. The doctor was amazed and asked: 'Did you follow my instructions?'

'Yes,' he said, 'but I thought I was going to drop dead on that third day.'

'From hunger, you mean?'

'No, from skipping!'

Two women friends went on a diet. One said: 'I entered what I ate yesterday into my new fitness app.'

'Well done you,' said the other. 'What did it say?'

'Nothing, but it sent an ambulance round to my house.'

Eighty-six-year-old Dorothy Densmore was arrested in 2005 for calling the emergency services because she was unable to get a single slice of pizza delivered to her apartment in Charlotte, North Carolina. She dialled 911 twenty times in less than half an hour and demanded that the police arrest the pizza parlour employee who had called her a 'crazy old coot' over the phone. When the police arrived to calm the situation, she allegedly bit the hand of an officer.

If we're not meant to creep downstairs for midnight snacks, why is there a light in the fridge?

'There isn't a problem on this earth that a doughnut cannot make better.'

ROSEANNE BARR

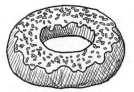

Becoming increasingly anxious about his growing weight, a man went to see a therapist. He told her that no matter how hard he tried, he never seemed able to stick to diets. After listening to his tale of anguish, she advised: 'The key to a happy and successful life is: always finish what you start.'

The man took these words on board and when he returned a week later for his next appointment, he had a much more optimistic outlook to life. 'I feel better already,' he told the therapist. 'So far today I've finished a family-size bag of crisps, a packet of chocolate cookies and a tub of ice cream.'

———

An elderly couple died within a few days of each other and were shown around heaven by St Peter. It was a fantastic place – permanent sunshine, swimming pools, bars, golf courses and tennis courts. 'Dammit, Edna,' hissed the husband, 'we could have been here ten years ago if you hadn't read about all those fancy low-fat diets.'

––––––––

The healthiest part of a doughnut is the hole. Even medical experts agree that you will not put on weight from eating the hole. So you shouldn't blame yourself for the fact that, because of a basic design fault, you have to eat your way through the rest of the doughnut in order to get to the healthy bit.

> *Impatient Inverness, Florida, police chief Joseph Elizade was forced to resign after arresting the proprietor of a Happy Days diner who had told him that the two hamburgers ordered twenty minutes earlier were still not ready.*

A man took his young daughter to the grocery store where, in addition to the meticulously prepared list of healthy items he had been ordered to get, he could not resist buying a box of sugar-rich cookies.

When they arrived home and unpacked the items, his wife immediately glared accusingly at the cookies.

'It's okay, darling,' he said reassuringly. 'This box

of cookies only has half as many calories as a usual box.'

'How come?' she asked.

'Because we ate half on the way home.'

————

A homeless person approached an elegant woman in the street and said: 'I haven't eaten anything in three days.'

'Gosh,' she said. 'I wish I had your willpower.'

————

HEALTH FOODS

And suddenly we're meant to care about health foods. Who decided? And that we're actually meant to give up meat. So why – please tell me – did we fight our way to the top of the food chain just to be a vegetarian? If anything is going to give you the grumps then it's sanctimonious prattle about quinoa, couscous and hummus, which is fine if you have ever had a craving for eating wallpaper paste. And don't even mention meat substitute, which essentially translates as 'flavourless'. What's the point of a sausage that doesn't taste like a sausage? Do people really eat sausages purely for the shape? And whoever got excited about eating lentils? What child in history has ever said: 'What's for dinner tonight, Mum? I do hope it's lentils again. They're so much more nutritious and wholesome than burgers and ice cream.'

Always remember:

* It's all very well eating plenty of natural foods, but think on, most people die of natural causes.

* Health food would seem healthier if the people who sold it looked less unhealthy.

* Healthy snack bars are for people who have ever wondered what it was like to pay way over the odds for something.

* Muesli is fine for breakfast – if you're a rabbit.

* Isn't it ironic that your 'salad days' refer to the best days of your life? You've led a sad life if your most joyous experience was eating a lettuce leaf.

* Following a strict vegan diet may not necessarily help you live longer, but it will certainly feel like it.

* If we are not supposed to eat animals, why does meat taste so good?

———

'You can either choose to be a vegan or you can choose to enjoy life.'

ROMESH RANGANATHAN

Bran is the only breakfast cereal where the cardboard box tastes better than the cereal itself. The great thing about bran is that you can accidentally drop a few pieces on the kitchen floor, tread on them with your slippers, and they will still taste the same.

———

Remember to eat at least five portions of fruit a day. So that's a chocolate orange, a sherbet lemon, a Hawaiian pizza (pineapple), a strawberry ice cream, and a doughnut containing raspberry jam . . . all washed down by a nice glass of peach schnapps.

*'The first time I tried organic wheat bread, I thought
I was chewing on roofing material.'*

ROBIN WILLIAMS

KEY RULES

So why does everyone keep bashing on about 'lose weight'. Why doesn't anyone champion obesity? Who wants to stand stark naked, look down and see their toes? I like looking at my pale grey, voluminous, hairy, perky stomach. And if you're greedy, here's why. Your partner is such an excellent cook. By devouring every last morsel on your plate – and theirs – you are being kind, appreciative. If they are the sort of cook who uses the smoke alarm as a timer, yes, things might be different. So basically the fact that you are marginally alarmingly overweight is not your fault. Remember this the next time you are about to devour an entire cow.

Moreover ...

* No self-respecting Grumpy would set foot in a McDonald's for fear of having to order a Happy Meal.

* The bad cook's motto: where there's smoke, there's dinner.

* It may just be that the answer to all of your problems could not be found at the bottom of that family-size tub of ice cream, but the important thing was that you tried.

———

'Pot Noodle: for best results, put back on the shelf.'

ANDY PARSONS

A wife served some homemade cinnamon rolls for breakfast and waited eagerly for her husband's reaction. When none was forthcoming, she asked him: 'If I baked these commercially, how much do you think I could get for one of them?'

Without looking up from his newspaper, he replied: 'About ten years.'

6

WHAT'S APP, DOC?

The younger generation are always telling us that we need to embrace modern technology. But when many of us can't tell an Xbox from a fuse box and think that a Twitter feed is a bird table, maybe it's all too much to take in. Mobile phones are very neat, but some of us still prefer a crackly landline and even get nostalgic about the days of shared party lines, when your conversation could suddenly be rudely interrupted by your neighbour from three doors down. What's the point of change? What's the point of computers and email and . . .

COMPUTERS – THE SEVEN KEY FACTS

1. There are only two kinds of computer – the latest model and the obsolete.

2. Your ideal computer comes on the market about two days after you have just bought another one.

3. A computer printer consists of three main parts: the case, the jammed paper tray and the blinking red light.

4. Your computer will always crash a split second before you remember to save the work you were doing on it.

5. The cause of most computer problems is the loose nut between the chair and the keyboard.

6. To err is human, but to really foul things up you really need a computer.

7. And how long do they take to install? Three days. Three weeks. My record – three years.

————

Officers at a military installation were being lectured about a sophisticated new computer. The training officer said it was able to withstand the most powerful nuclear and chemical attacks.

Just then he noticed that one of the officers was

holding a cup of coffee. 'Get out of here with that coffee!' he barked.

'Okay, but why?' asked the embarrassed officer.

'Because spilt coffee could ruin the keyboard.'

———

I bought my mum a Kindle because she likes reading so much. She still licks her fingers when she changes the page.

LEE EVANS

———

AND AS FOR THE INTERNET …

If a poor connection is giving you grief, you are left with little option but to call your broadband provider helpline, an experience like entering the Bermuda Triangle.

Adhering resolutely to their prepared script, the helpline advisors insist that any problem – even though they don't know what it is exactly – must be your fault. When you try to explain, patiently at first, that nothing has changed in your home setup to cause the connection to fail suddenly, they tell you that it must have done. 'Are

you sure you haven't demolished a wall of your house?' they demand.

You then spend six hours on and off the phone to them conducting a series of futile tests before they finally agree to send out an engineer, warning that you will have to pay for his visit. When the engineer does come – not at the agreed time but during the last over of the final Test Match – he plays with a few settings, says it's not your fault and that he will inform your broadband provider. There will be nothing to pay. You seriously think about changing provider, until you are reminded that you have been saying the same thing for the past nine years. Besides, to cancel you would need to get in touch with them, and you don't think you could bear to go through all that again.

———

'Ten years I've been Skyping my mother and I've never seen more than the top of her head.'

AISLING BEA

———

And note, you are spending too much time on the internet if:

* You've never actually met any of your friends.

* Your partner looks deep into your eyes and sees a screen saver.

* You can't talk to your mother because she's not on Skype.

* You have an identity crisis because someone is using a similar screen name to yours.

* You wake at three o'clock in the morning to go to the bathroom and, on your way back to bed, you stop to check your email.

* You haven't played solitaire with real cards in years.

* You refer to going to the bathroom as 'downloading'.

* You try to enter your computer password on the microwave.

* You spend an entire plane journey with your laptop on your lap and your child in the overhead baggage compartment.

* You turn on your computer and turn off your partner.

What's more:

* If your internet password is hacked, there is only one thing you can do: rename your cat.

* And why do they call it surfing the internet as if it's some athletic pursuit? It's nothing more than typing in the bedroom.

* Why would anyone want to play online poker? It's like being mugged but without the company.

* At our age one of the chief problems with the internet is that on some websites we can get finger cramp just by scrolling all the way down to find our year of birth.

* The only thing many of us could readily identify with on the internet was Grumpy Cat. Some days it was just like looking in the mirror.

* You can probably identify with computer hackers because you have often been tempted to take an axe to yours.

* Technology is deliberately designed to confuse us. In a moment when our mind was elsewhere, who hasn't been on the point of trying to toast a sandwich in a laptop?

* A TV can insult your intelligence, but nothing rubs it in like a computer.

Annoyed at being unable to obtain a decent internet connection, a customer phoned his provider's technical support department. He outlined the problem but the voice on the other end responded with terms and abbreviations that were so obscure they could have come from the planet Zog.

Eventually in frustration, the customer said: 'Sorry, I don't understand a word you are saying. Can you explain to me what I should do as if I were a small child?'

'Okay,' said the tech support man slowly. 'Please – can – you – put – your – mummy – on the – phone?'

———

EMAIL, THEY SAY . . .

. . . is so much easier than the phone, but when you send an email you have no idea whether it has reached its destination. So unless you receive a reply, you probably end up phoning the person anyway to check that they've received the email.

Junk mail or spam is the curse of the internet, bombarding you with messages ranging from needy Nigerian princes who can make you wealthy beyond your dreams (if you just transfer funds to their account) to impossibly beautiful Russian women living in your area who are apparently very keen to meet you – even though you are sixty-six, overweight and the only thing you can attract on a regular basis is dandruff.

Then there is 'selected' mail that you might receive after you have made a purchase online. When you come to pay, there is a box that you can tick or untick in order to receive (or refuse) emails from 'relevant third parties'. Giving you the choice in the matter sounds admirable, but the wording next to the box often appears deliberately designed to trap you, incorporating double negatives at will so that you have to read it several times before you can be sure whether you are actually permitting or rejecting this third party mail. And who decides what is 'relevant'? Every time you shop at a certain online garden centre you receive an email the next day from a funeral company. Just because you've recently bought daisies doesn't mean you're ready to push them up.

And remember: email is for communicating with people to whom you would rather not talk.

With their relationship going through a rough patch, a woman began to despair of ever getting her husband to open up to her. She was becoming increasingly concerned that he was spending more time on his laptop than he was with her. Finally her frustration boiled over and she told him in no uncertain terms: 'We need to communicate more.'

'You're absolutely right,' he conceded. 'I'll send you my email address.'

———

How can you stop your husband reading your email? Rename the email folder 'Instruction manual'.

THE MODERN CURSE

Yes, the mobile phone. They are all very well for young people with their spider-thin, fast-texting fingers, but with our fat, clumsy porkers . . . When you read the message back, it looks as if it's written in Polish. So then you have to re-do it S-L-O-W-L-Y and carefully, and by the time you've done that it would have been quicker to make a call or even send the message by pigeon. And never trust predictive text to convey your true feelings. The message 'Happy birthday dear husband' can easily be sent by the unwary as 'Happy birthday dead husband'. Or 'Grandad is home from hospital' can end up as 'Grandad is homosexual'. Arguing with autocorrect is the new yelling at the television.

'The mobile phone, the fax machine, email: call me old-fashioned, but what's wrong with a chain of beacons?'

HARRY HILL

AND storing all of your photographs on your mobile phone has apparently made life so much easier. Yes, easier, for people to bore you rigid with their holiday

snaps or the latest picture of their dog behaving . . . like a dog. There is no escape. You are a captive audience at the mercy of modern technology. At least in our day if we wanted to bore someone for hours on end with holiday memories, we either had to bring out the dusty old photo album from the cupboard above the wardrobe or kick the slide projector into life, when a third of the slides would be the wrong way up and we all had to crane our necks at an angle of ninety degrees to see what was going on.

Smartphones ...

* Specifically designed to be slim enough to slip down the side of the sofa and not be seen again for months.

* Have completely killed the art of conversation. Nobody talks to each other anymore – they've all got their face in their phone. These days the only way to get your teenage son to pass the gravy at the dinner table is to text him.

* Anyone with a novelty ring tone on their phone is merely trying to bring a swift conclusion to the debate as to whether or not, in this great world of ours, they are a complete waste of space.

* The screens are so small that it's difficult to read the writing without your glasses. It's easy to think you keep getting messages or missed calls from someone called Betty Low, only to realise it says 'Battery Low'.

* And why do people get so excited about their smartphones? All they did was buy one, they didn't invent it!

————

ONLINE DATING IS . . .

. . . as romantic as buying false teeth on Amazon. Are we oldies really meant to conjure up a twinkly new mate through a battered aluminium box? And then, of course, who tells the truth, so when you finally meet them in the flesh (*caveat emptor*), the 'six-foot-tall James Bond lookalike' turns out to be a midget with a comb-over. Online dating profiles use as much poetic licence as estate agents; need a translation?

Bubbly = *loud*
Enjoys quiet nights in = *tight with money*
A bit crazy = *boring as hell*
Steady and reliable = *still lives at home with elderly mother*
Easy going = *indecisive*
Searching for my soulmate = *scarily intense*

Great personality = *nothing to look at*

Suave and distinguished = *can use a knife and fork without spilling too much down his tie*

I'm looking for good banter = *coarse misogynist*

Successful businessman = *branch manager at McDonald's*

Cuddly = *obese*

I work out a lot = *I'm obsessed with my body*

Happy-go-lucky = *irresponsible*

Free spirit = *certifiable*

I'm shy when it comes to talking about myself = *I have a criminal record*

My profile picture is old = *it's a picture of someone else*

Plus with online dating there is always the fear that in your excitement you are going to swipe the wrong way, and that you may have inadvertently arranged to spend an evening in the company of a man whose hobbies include trainspotting, collecting his toenail clippings and breeding maggots.

When a Los Angeles man advertised as a lonely Romeo looking for someone to accompany him on a trip to South America, the first reply he received was from his widowed mother.

———————

Trapped in a miserable marriage, Sana and Adnan Klaric sought love in internet chat rooms, only to end up romancing each other online under false names. The couple, from Zenica, Bosnia, met on an online forum while she was in an internet café and he was at work, and began chatting under the names 'Sweetie' and 'Prince of Joy'.

After pouring out their hearts to one another about their marriage problems, they eventually arranged to meet outside a shop, each carrying a single rose for identification. But there was no happy ending when they realized what had happened. Instead both filed for divorce, with each accusing the other of being unfaithful. Adnan lamented: 'I still find it hard to believe that Sweetie, who wrote such wonderful things to me on the internet, is actually the same woman I married and who has not said a nice word to me for years.'

Ten-year-old Zoe Pemberton, from Clacton, Essex, put her 'moaning' grandmother up for sale on eBay – and was offered 3,000 dollars for her before the auction was halted. Although she loved her dearly, Zoe described grandma Marion Goodall as 'rare and annoying and moaning a lot'.

FACEBOOK

Don't get me started. The adult way of having imaginary friends. As soon as you join – when you have given nothing more than your name and location – you are informed that all manner of total strangers would like to be your friend. Where were these people when you needed that loan last year? All Facebook does is show old schoolmates that you haven't aged as well as them. You end up feeling even grumpier than usual because everyone else seems to be having a much better time than you. In truth, that's only because people tend not to mention their bankruptcy or fallen arches on Facebook. Furthermore, once we could be painfully boring in private; social media has changed all that.

'Can we go back to using Facebook for what it was originally for – looking up exes to see how fat they got.'

BILL MAHER

TWITTER

Is something of a curate's egg for we Grumps stuck in the eighteenth century. While the perpetual sense of moral indignation exploding into downright outrage may align with our nature, making it very much a mouthpiece for miserable old gits, having to restrict ourselves to two hundred and eighty characters to express our fury does present a problem. Let's face it, most of us ramble on so much that we can't tell anyone what the time is in fewer than two hundred and eighty characters.

————

There was a time when people regularly thought of something really pointless to say but would then think better of it in case they made themselves look stupid. Then along came Twitter.

————

'There's something very macho about how many followers you have on Twitter. Jesus had followers but he had something important to say, not "Had a bath, watched Sex and the City.*"'*

SEAN LOCK

————

Why do they describe something as 'new and improved', which is it? If it's new, there has never been anything before it. If it's an improvement, there must have been something before it. They can't have it both ways.

————

SIRI, ALEXA, YOU NAME IT

No sooner does the Modern just about become acceptable, they throw in Siri and Alexa. Apparently, these idiotic contraptions can turn on the lights (in case you have suddenly forgotten how light switches work), find a recipe (but not actually make it) and tell you what the weather is like at any given time in Uzbekistan. But ask it to fetch you a beer from the fridge and it won't move an inch. In fact,

it's more likely to ask if you want to 'peer from a bridge'. 'Sydney Harbour has excellent visibility today, and the temperature is a pleasant twenty-two degrees.' NO!!

You can also download extra Alexa skills, including one that simulates the sound of someone snoring next to you through the night. This feature is supposed to provide comfort and relieve loneliness, but if you live alone would you really want to wake up suddenly in the middle of the night, terrified that a stranger has climbed into your bed? And if you don't live alone, the last thing you want to hear all night is your partner snoring. Dream on, Alexa.

IPOD–ISHMOD

Who, yes WHO, needs thirty thousand songs? You probably have a collection of about fifty CDs (plus a few tapes gathering dust in a neglected box), of which you only like half. The rest were either free offers or seemed like a good idea at the time. And anyway, so what if you can listen to music all day long on an iPod and even shuffle the order so that you don't know what's coming next? There's another device that allows you to do that and it's been around for years. The RADIO.

ATMs

I liked my bank. They liked me. And the lady cashier clearly had a Big Twinkly for me. (The way she lisped, 'What can I do for *you*, Mr…') But now, ATMs. What, you ask, is the problem? Where do I begin? Too many questions (What is your PIN? How much money do you want? Do you want to know your balance? Do you want a receipt?). I say … 'Mind your own business.'

Those of us who are particularly cautious tend to use the same ATM over and over again, we need to have a rapport. If it is unexpectedly out of use and we have to go to a *different* machine, we become a nervous wreck for the rest of the day until we can check our balance and be sure that it's not a rogue ATM that has emptied our account.

Also, cash machines are frequented by two irritating types of people. First, the dawdlers who take forever to press the keys and count their money afterwards. They are the sort of people who treat a visit to an ATM as a day out. It's a wonder they don't bring some sandwiches and a flask of coffee. Then there are those who insist on standing right behind you while you are keying in your PIN. The best response is to turn around, look them in the eye and march them back three yards, like a referee awarding a foul. Unless, of course, they are bigger than you.

SHOPPING

I last enjoyed shopping in 1947. Nowadays, they try to interest you in a loyalty card. But your wallet is bulging enough already with pieces of plastic, so the last thing you need is yet another card. As a result of the overcrowding, cards inevitably slide behind one another or you become confused as to which card does what. Who hasn't tried to board a bus with a supermarket reward card or pay a restaurant bill with a library card? No? You will.

And as for buying clothes. Without sending us a personal apology beforehand, the store has suddenly decided to stop selling the same type of baggy, aerated Y-fronts that we have been buying for the past seventy-eight years. We moan that all the sizing must be wrong because we are never an extra large; at the exorbitant prices; and we moan that it is now almost impossible to buy long socks unless you are going on a Himalayan expedition. In winter, who wants socks that barely cover your ankles?

Food shopping is no better, and we draw the line at using the self-service supermarket checkout. Although these machines have allegedly become more user-friendly, despite that dreaded message about an 'unexpected item

in the bagging area', they are still a potential disaster zone for the unwary. For example, you can easily lose a hand while trying to help a bank note into the payment slot. And as for correctly identifying fruit and vegetables on the touch screen...

Now, most of us can still distinguish between an orange and a grapefruit but put pictures of them on a screen and the mind goes AWOL, especially if there is a marked price difference between the two. We don't want to key in the more expensive fruit in case we are paying for something we haven't bought, but if we key in the cheaper fruit and it turns out to be wrong, we'll be apprehended by store security on the way out.

The trouble with machines is that you simply can't reason with them. Besides, we miss the friendly repartee with the human behind the till, like 'Why aren't there more tills open – can't you see there are people waiting?' 'Why haven't you got any large pineapples this week?' and 'I'm not paying full price for this – there's a bruise on it.'

TRAVEL AND ... TAKING ORDERS

GPS systems are apparently very popular with the young, but if you really want to hear a dispassionate voice firing out directions in your car, you can always give your teenage son another lift to his friend's house. Anyway, what's wrong with good old-fashioned map reading? You know where you are with a map – well, most of the time. And only a proper map can tell you essential information like whether or not the next village has a church with a tower or whether there is a fourteenth-century battlefield in the vicinity. In any case, SatNav systems are by no means infallible ...

A Syrian truck driver transporting luxury cars from Turkey to Gibraltar on the southern tip of Spain was sent on a 1,600-mile detour to England by his satellite navigation system. Birdwatchers at Gibraltar Point in Lincolnshire looked on in astonishment as Necdet Bakimci tried to steer his thirty-two-ton truck down a narrow country lane towards the North Sea. When questioned, he explained that he was looking for Gibraltar on mainland Europe. It is thought the confusion arose because his device had listed Gibraltar as UK territory and so directed him towards Britain.

AND CHANGING THE SUBJECT (AS WE DO)

* A reclining chair might sound like a modern gadget worth buying until you realize that you have to plug it in. So basically it's an electric chair.

* Even the grumpiest old git would accept – albeit grudgingly – that colour television has been a step worth making from black and white. But do we really need HD TV? They say it's almost like having the people on screen in your front room. Frankly, the day you find Piers Morgan in your front room is the day you move house.

* Do you know why they call the TV control a remote? It's because, at any given time, most of us don't have the remotest idea where the damn thing is.

* Adolescence is a time of rapid change. Between the ages of thirteen and nineteen, a parent can age as much as twenty years.

* A millennial is always too tired to hold a tea towel, but never too tired to hold a phone.

Q: What's the best way to keep a teenage boy out of hot water? A: Put some dishes in it.

At the end of thirteen years writing a weighty tome about the Swedish economy, business consultant Ulf af Trolle finally took his 252-page manuscript to be copied. Alas, it took only seconds for his life's work to be reduced to 50,000 strips of paper when an employee confused the copier with the shredder.

———

A woman was subjected to a harrowing two-hour ordeal when she was 'imprisoned' in a hi-tech public toilet. Maureen Shotton was captured by the maverick cyberloo during a shopping trip to Newcastle upon Tyne. The toilet, which boasted state-of-the-art electronic auto-flush and door sensors, steadfastly refused to release her and resisted all attempts by passers-by to force the door. She was finally freed when firefighters ripped the roof off the toilet.

———

An adulterous Finn pressed all the wrong buttons as he made love in a car, unwittingly prompting his mobile phone to call home just in time for his wife to hear his mistress moan: 'I love you.' When he later arrived home, his wife attacked him with an axe.

7

BEAUTY IS IN THE EYE OF THE BEERHOLDER

It's outrageous: cutting back our alcohol intake is now recommended for improving both our health and general wellbeing. Who decided that? And without a drink or two we would be even grumpier. The prospect of a refreshing beer or a perky glass of wine (tip: try a Hungarian furmint) is what gets us through the week. It's true that we need a clear head to deal with nemeses such as call centres, insurance companies and our bank, but it's equally true that we need a stiff drink afterwards. Cheers!

SEVEN POINTS IN PRAISE OF BEER

1. Love is a beautiful four-letter word . . . as is beer.

2. They say money can't buy you happiness, but it can if you use it to buy beer.

3. Life and beer are very similar. Chill for best results.

4. Beer: it's not just for breakfast anymore.

5. A beer in the hand is worth two in the fridge.

6. Drinking beer doesn't make you fat. It makes you lean – against bars, walls, stools. . .

7. Meditation is not evasion; it is a serene encounter with reality. The same goes for beer.

After a few drinks too many, a man staggered into a Catholic church and ended up in the confession booth. Following a short period of silence, the priest asked quietly: 'What do you need, my son?'

The man said: 'There's no paper on my side. Is there any on yours?'

———

A man asked his friend: 'Would you care for a beer?' The friend replied: 'Like it was my own mother.'

A defendant stood before the judge in court. The judge said solemnly: 'You've been brought here for drinking. 'Great', said the defendant. 'Let's get started.'

'When I read about the evils of drinking, I gave up reading.'

HENNY YOUNGMAN

'A woman drove me to drink, and I didn't even have the decency to thank her.'

W.C. FIELDS

'Without question, the greatest invention in the history of mankind is beer. Oh, I grant you that the wheel was also a fine invention, but the wheel does not go nearly as well with pizza.'

DAVE BARRY

THE SACRED TENETS OF DRINKING

There's more to drink than just beer. A snorter, a noggin, potions, giggle juice ...

* You ought to feel sorry for people who don't drink. When they wake up in the morning, that's as good as they're going to feel all day.

* If alcohol isn't the answer, who cares what the question is?

* Lead me not into temptation. I can find the way myself.

* Everyone has their own path in life. Fortunately yours leads to the liquor store.

* Alcohol is like pouring smiles onto your brain.

* Don't let yourself believe that you have an alcohol addiction; think of it more as an alcohol dedication.

* If someone accuses you of being a hard drinker, correct them instantly. Tell them you actually find it very easy.

* You drink to make other people interesting.

* Only drink on days beginning with a T – that's Tuesday, Thursday, today and tomorrow.

* Always take life with a pinch of salt . . . plus a slice of lime and a shot of tequila.

* Tequila may not fix your life, but it's worth a shot.

* It's always good to cook with wine. Sometimes you can even put it in the food.

* Your New Year's resolution should be to be more optimistic by keeping your glass half full – whether it's with whisky, rum or vodka.

A man staggered home to find his wife waiting for him. 'What do you think you're doing coming home half drunk?' she bellowed.

'Sorry,' he replied. 'I ran out of money.'

—————

A woman was still angry the morning after a party. She told her husband: 'You certainly made a fool of yourself last night. I just hope nobody realized you were sober.'

'There are better things in life than alcohol, but it makes up for not having them.'

TERRY PRATCHETT

A man who was decidedly the worse for drink was wandering along the street at five o'clock in the morning. A police officer stopped him and said: 'Can you explain why you're out at this hour?'

The man replied: 'If I could, I'd be home by now!'

Having just turned sixty, a man went to see his doctor for his first annual health check. The doctor began by asking him questions about his lifestyle.

'Do you drink to excess?' asked the doctor.

The man replied: 'I'll drink to anything!'

A woman was rushing home from work when she was stopped in the street by a market researcher.

'Do you drink alcohol?' asked the researcher.

'Yes, I do,' answered the woman, trying to escape.

'Any particular sort?'

'I'm very partial to a bottle of wine.'

'And what do you spend on a bottle of wine?'

'Oh, about half an hour.'

———

Arriving home drunk one night, a husband cut himself when he walked into a shelf by the front door. With blood trickling down his face, he went straight upstairs to the bathroom to carry out repairs to his wounds.

The next morning his wife said: 'You came home drunk last night, didn't you?'

'No,' he replied, lying through his teeth.

'Then perhaps you can explain why there are plasters all over the bathroom mirror?'

TOO YOUNG OR TOO OLD?

To buy alcohol you've got to be over eighteen in the UK and twenty-one in the United States. Fine. No problem. But the way it is enforced by stores . . . When did that start? Staff even grill OAPs on zimmer frames: 'Are you over eighteen? Prove it.' You think I'm joking? Read on . . .

A supermarket on The Wirral in England refused to serve alcohol to seventy-two-year-old Tony Ralls because he would not confirm that he was over twenty-one, the age specified by a scheme that the store was operating. The white-haired grandfather-of-three had tried to buy two bottles of wine but when asked to confirm that he was old enough to purchase alcohol he refused, saying that it was a 'stupid question'. Instead he asked to see the manager who promptly put the bottles back on the shelf. The irate pensioner abandoned his shopping and left the store, demanding an apology.

OVER CAFFEINATED

Too much coffee can be every bit as bad for you as alcohol. Here's how you can detect if you have exceeded your recommended intake of caffeine:

* You haven't blinked since the last lunar eclipse.

* You can ski uphill.

* You can jump-start your car without cables.

* You chew on other people's fingernails.

* You sleep with your eyes open.

* People get dizzy just from watching you.

* Instead of sweating, you percolate.

* You help your dog chase its tail.

* You can only watch DVDs on fast-forward.

* You soak your dentures overnight in coffee.

* Instant coffee takes too long.

* There's a picture of your coffee mug on your coffee mug.

Having had one too many drinks for the road at his local bar, Wolfgang Heinrich decided to sleep it off for the night by riding his horse into a German bank. He had been out riding his horse Sammy when he stopped to have a drink with friends, but on leaving the bar he realized he was too drunk to ride all the way back to his home in Wiesenburg. So, keen to get out of the cold, he used his bank card to open up the local branch of the Mittelbrandenburgische Sparkasse and take himself and Sammy inside for the night. Heinrich was found fast asleep with his horse by customer Stephan Hanelt, who went to the bank to withdraw money early the following morning. With commendable understatement, Hanelt said: 'It was a bit of a shock to find a man and horse asleep in the foyer of the bank.' He called the police who let Heinrich off with a warning. Bank staff were less amused when they had to clean up after Sammy, who had left a deposit of his own on the foyer floor.

8

IF ALL THINGS ARE POSSIBLE, TRY SKIING THROUGH A REVOLVING DOOR

Who appointed the thought police? Did the great Victorians have them? The Edwardians? So why are we now repeatedly told that when we are negative we can kiss goodbye to our hopes and dreams. What preposterous . . . The Big Bad Wolf was positive; he huffed and he puffed, but his inability to grasp even the basics of structural engineering meant that his quest for bacon was doomed to end in abject failure. Negativity is highly under-valued. The young haven't got a clue. Why are they all so cheery?

Yes, a lifetime's experience has taught us that optimism

is invariably misplaced. Remember the horse that couldn't possibly lose (which was so far behind the rest of the field that they had to send out a search party), the four-bedroom house in a quiet location (which turned out to be next to the cemetery), the top-of-the range wedding buffet (which consisted of a plain cheese sandwich, a cowpat of a sausage on a stick, a pickled onion, four potato crisps and as much salad as you could eat), and the jackpot prize draw that promised we were definitely among the last six in line to win half a million (only to reveal at the last minute, after we had jumped through endless hoops, that all we had won was a cheap pen). Forget all that. Grumpies live by – relish – Murphy's Law and its cynical cousin Sod's Law, which in effect states that anything that can go wrong will go wrong. And that's our default position, our defence against today's politically correct, hectoring optimism.

If you want sanity, try these quotes. Do you think these guys got it right all the time?

> *'Blessed is the man who expects nothing, for he shall never be disappointed.'*
>
> ALEXANDER POPE

'I try to look on the bright side, but it really hurts my eyes.'

DANA GOULD

———

'Both optimists and pessimists contribute to society. The optimist invents the aeroplane, the pessimist the parachute.'

GEORGE BERNARD SHAW

———

'I'd like to leave you with something positive, but I can't think of anything positive to say. Would you take two negatives?'

WOODY ALLEN

———

APHORISMS TO LIVE BY (1)

* Good news is just life's way of keeping you off balance.

* Today may be the first day of the rest of your life, but equally it's also the last day of your life so far.

* Every morning is the dawn of a new error.

* I believe that for every drop of rain that falls . . . someone gets wet.

* Into every life some rain must fall – usually when your car roof is down.

* The only time the world beats a path to your door is when you're in the bathroom.

* Remember when one door closes, another slams in your face.

* Opportunities always look bigger going than coming.

* Things are never so bad that a politician can't make them worse.

* The world will end the day after the warranty expires.

* If everything's coming your way, you're probably driving on the wrong side of the road.

* All inanimate objects can move just enough to get in your way.

* The most affectionate creature in the world is a wet dog.

* If something is confidential, it will be left in the photocopier.

* Smile. Tomorrow will be worse.

My father used to say: 'When one door closes, another one opens.' Whereas my mother used to say: 'Jack, isn't it about time you got that car fixed? It's embarrassing.'

———

'A husband was late home from work one evening. 'I'm sure he's having an affair,' said his wife to her mother.

'Why do you always think the worst?' said the mother. 'Maybe he's been in a car crash.'

McArthur Wheeler was positive that by smearing lemon juice on his face while he robbed two Pittsburgh banks one day in 1995 he would be invisible to security cameras. After all, lemon juice is used as invisible ink, so what could possibly go wrong? There was no need to wear a mask, he reasoned. The juice would do the trick. To demonstrate his unshakeable confidence in the plan, he even smiled at surveillance cameras before walking out of each bank. When he was arrested later that day and police officers showed him the clear security camera pictures of his face at both banks, he could only stare in disbelief, mumbling: 'But I wore the juice.'

APHORISMS TO LIVE BY (2)

* Every time you find the meaning of life, they change it.

* Just when you think you've won the rat race, along come faster rats.

* Experience is that wonderful thing that allows you to recognize a mistake when you make it again.

* Rely on the rabbit's foot if you must, but remember – it didn't work for the rabbit.

* When it's you against the world, I'd bet on the world.

* Whatever hits the fan will not be evenly distributed.

* Anything you lose will be in the last place you look for it.

* Remember, the light at the end of the tunnel could just as easily be an oncoming train.

* Talk is cheap until you hire a lawyer.

* It's a small world until you chase your hat down the street.

* A bird in the hand makes blowing your nose difficult.

* The shin bone is a device for finding furniture in a dark room.

When police detectives in London were struggling to execute a search warrant on a house with a solid steel door, PC Dean Cunnington decided to act positively by volunteering to borrow a postman's uniform and knock on the door in disguise. Hearing the knock, a voice inside the house called out: 'Who is it?'

'It's the police,' replied PC Cunnington.

———

Hannes Pisek calculated that he needed to make a big romantic gesture to impress his girlfriend. So, thinking positively, he made a giant heart out of 220 candles on the floor of his apartment in Hoenigsberg, Austria. He then lit them and went to collect his beloved from work. However, his hopes of a romantic evening were dashed when the apartment caught fire in his absence. He not only lost his home but also his girlfriend who promptly dumped him and moved back in with her parents.

NEW YEAR, NEW YOU – BAH!

There are certain things that never change. Why fight them? Resistance is futile! Better to accept them and live up to your grumpy reputation:

* The only time your local bus is running a minute early coincides with the only time you are running a minute late.

* Any tool, when dropped, will roll to the least accessible corner.

* The more expensive the wedding, the quicker the divorce.

* The more expensive the plant, and the greater amount of care and attention that you lavish upon it, the quicker it will shrivel up and die.

* The other queue always moves faster. And if you decide, in frustration, to change queues, the one you were in will always move faster than the one you are in now.

* The severity of the itch is directly proportional to the reach.

* A flying particle will seek the nearest eye. This is especially true of grapefruit juice, which can be relied upon to hit your eye with unerring accuracy.

* The flat screen TV you paid full price for will be in a sale the day after.

* Just when you think you've reached rock bottom, someone hands you a shovel.

* Birds of a feather flock together and crap on your car.

* The only time in your life that you get spinach stuck in your teeth is when you are sitting opposite someone you are trying to impress.

* Your lost needle will be found by your husband while he is walking around the house barefoot.

* The easiest way to find something lost around the house is to buy a replacement.

* The items in a shoe sale will be in every size except yours.

* When a broken appliance is demonstrated for the repairman, it will work perfectly – and then break down again when he has left.

* Any repairman will never have seen a model like yours before.

* Remember, no one is listening until you fart.

* Also remember the 50/50-90 rule: anytime you have a 50/50 chance of getting something right, there is a 90 per cent probability that you will get it wrong.

When Stan Caddell wanted to wash his Chevrolet and save money, he decided to invoke the power of positive thinking. He was confident that he would be able to wash his car in the Mississippi River instead, thereby avoiding having to pay for a car wash. So he carefully backed the car into one foot of water at Hannibal, Missouri, but no sooner had he climbed out to clean it than the car floated away. Police eventually managed to retrieve the vehicle some distance down river. An officer attending the incident confirmed that no action would be taken against Caddell because 'you can't ticket a guy for being stupid'.

GLASS HALF FULL?

Can we really change our ways? If you're a natural grump, can you really be expected to shuck off the pessimist in you . . . or is it actually healthier to stay exactly as you are, new year or not?

An optimist and a pessimist were best friends. For years, the optimist had been trying to get the pessimist to say something positive but always without success. Then one day the optimist had the bright idea of buying a pet so talented that even the pessimist would be unable to find fault with it. So he went to the local pet shop and asked the owner whether he had any birds or animals with a remarkable talent.

'I have a dog that can walk on water,' said the pet shop owner.

'Perfect,' said the optimist. 'I'll take him. My friend won't be able to say anything negative about such an amazing dog.'

The next day, the optimist and his new dog went for a walk by the lake with the pessimist. The optimist was playing catch with the dog on the bank but then suddenly he hurled the ball out into the middle of the lake. Just as the store owner had promised, the dog stood on its back legs, ran across the water, fetched the ball and ran back across the water to shore.

Grinning from ear to ear, the optimist turned to his friend and asked: 'Notice anything unusual about my dog?'

'Sure,' said the pessimist. 'He can't swim.'

* Always borrow money from pessimists – they don't expect it back.

* You know you're a pessimist when your blood type is B Negative.

* You know you're a pessimist when opportunity only knocks on your door to complain about the noise.

* A pessimist is a man who looks both ways before crossing a one-way street.

* If you had a pound for every time someone called you a pessimist, you still probably wouldn't be able to afford anything worthwhile.

Q: How do you know when you've walked into the annual meeting of the Society of Pessimists?
A: The room is half-empty.

'An optimist is simply a pessimist with no job experience.'

SCOTT ADAMS

* An optimist is a driver who thinks that empty space at the kerb won't have a hydrant beside it.

* An optimist is someone who fills in a crossword puzzle in ink.

* An optimist is someone who believes that an escalator can never break – it can only become stairs.

* Unbridled optimism is a dangerous beast. Always exercise a degree of caution. So even on the sunniest of days, don't forget your umbrella.

* Remember, if something seems too good to be true, it probably is.

* Even at a Mensa convention, someone has to be the dumbest person in the room.

When tax inspectors raided a Buenos Aires textile sweatshop, everybody ran away except for one man who was positive that he would be able to avoid capture by posing as an elegant female mannequin. Hurriedly slipping on a dress, he stood motionless in the hope that nobody would see through his cunning disguise. He might have got away with it but for the fact that he was still wearing a pair of large scruffy sandals.

9

GETTING DOWN WITH THE KIDS

Nothing's more likely to make a Grump explode than mention of the young. Everything they do is *different*. Why? Attention seeking, jumped up BABOONS. An alien species, they speak a strange language, listen to stuff that barely qualifies as music and wear jeans that are actually designed with huge holes in them. Yes, we helped raise them but the best thing we can do is disown and DISINHERIT. Note: growing pains – are they something teenagers have or something teenagers are?

If a Grump attempts to engage with *them*, we face an immediate problem – the language barrier. They appear to have given up on English as we know it, instead devising their own slang made up of acronyms, abbreviations and words that mean whatever they want them to. So it's best not to attempt yoofspeak. Consequently, 'unreal' should only be used to describe the likes of artificial grass or the Loch Ness Monster, 'chilled' should only be used to describe the contents of the fridge freezer and 'hip' should only be used when followed by the word 'replacement'. Here are a few mystifying examples:

* When your son describes his girlfriend as 'a keeper', it does not necessarily mean that she works in a zoo.

* Bizarrely, 'wicked' means 'really good' as opposed to 'really bad'.

* A 'snack' refers to a particularly attractive man or woman, so expect barely stifled giggles when telling a teenage person that you sometimes fancy a snack in the middle of the night.

* An 'earworm' is not a medical condition, but a song that becomes stuck in your head, and not always for the right reasons.

* 'Gassed' means 'funny' or 'exciting'. Why?

* 'GOAT' is an acronym for 'Greatest of all Time' but not necessarily the greatest goat of all time.

* 'Burger' apparently means 'cool' or 'awesome', so presumably there can be such a thing as a 'burger burger'. Oh, for heaven's sake, why can't they just speak normal English?

So when young people moan that we don't understand them, they're right. We really don't. The way to counteract modern slang in conversation with them is to use arcane expressions of our own. Try slipping in phrases such as 'You could have knocked me down with a feather' or 'Well, I'll go to the foot of our stairs' and enjoy the look of bewilderment on their faces. After that, with any luck they'll stop trying to talk to you altogether.

TROUBLESOME TEENS

The trouble with teenagers is:

> * They are incredibly well informed about any
>   subject they don't have to study.

* Argumentative teenagers are always saying, 'You've got to meet me halfway', except when they're expecting a lift home.

* Their hang-ups don't include clothes.

PS: When your kids are teenagers, it is important to have a dog so that at least one member of the household is happy to see you.

PPS: Mother Nature is wonderful. She gives us twelve years to develop a love for our children before turning them into teenagers.

———

'Teenagers are obviously God's punishment for having sex in the first place.'

KATHY LETTE

———

MONEY AND CLOTHES

One of the most maddening things about the young and virile is that they have no idea of getting their money's worth. If they buy a pair of shoes that for some bizarre reason they don't like, they simply *throw* them out. We, on the other hand, who understand RAGE, and have bought a pair of shoes that turn out to be so uncomfortable that they reduce us to a limping wreck within a hundred yards, stoically battle through the pain barrier and wear them a few more times so that our investment is not totally wasted. That's called 'having a life'.

Ah yes, and never be tempted to demonstrate your youth credentials by dressing like *them*. The 'urban gangsta' look is notoriously difficult to carry off when completed with a cardigan and sensible shoes. All of these are a definite no-no:

* A baseball cap, especially when worn backwards. You will simply look like someone who can't be trusted to dress himself properly in the morning.

* Cargo pants or anything too low-slung, because nobody – absolutely nobody – wants to see your butt cleavage at an age when, rather than resembling two perky young Labradors, it looks more like a pair of jowly bloodhounds.

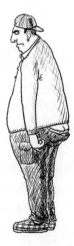

* Ripped jeans, because holes in jeans should only ever be the result of wear and tear.

* Nose piercings. With one in each nostril, you will look less like urban chic and more like bait.

* Nipple rings. Quite apart from looking ridiculous at your age, they can present a considerable health hazard if you find yourself unexpectedly close to a large magnet.

* Tattoos. Let's be honest, the only older man who has ever looked remotely acceptable with a tattoo is Popeye. And tattoos do not sit well with beer guts. As your stomach expands, what started out as a tattoo of a small, single rose can look more like a forest. Also, if your tattoo contains a mistake, you can be left with it for the rest of your life.

Tattoos in Chinese characters have become increasingly popular, but the recipients do not always get what they asked for. One man asked for a Chinese tattoo on his chest to express the words 'To find happiness', but instead the translation came out as 'I am slow'. Another requested 'Fear no man' on his arm, but the resultant Chinese tattoo read 'Coffin man'. Don't say you haven't been warned.

VIDEO GAMES ... AND THAT'S NOT WHAT I CALL MUSIC

Spend time with the grandchildren and they expect you to zap and kill. The world is going bonkers. Don't they enjoy the sheer boredom of doing a jigsaw? And then suddenly the sproggets are at a treatment centre for video game addiction. (And do tell them, you must fit all the jigsaw edge pieces first before you are allowed to build inwards, but that's just standard protocol. Disregard it at your peril.)

And as for music. We had folk, jazz, pop/rock and classical. That was it. Herman's Hermits or Handel. Now it is estimated that there are more than 1,200 genres of modern music, with names like charred death, hard glam, vaporwave, electro trash and deep filthstep. And we wonder why the world is going to rack and ruin.

Of course, most of this stuff isn't music at all – it's just noise, as you can tell if you ever have the misfortune to hear it emanating from somebody's headphones on the bus or blaring out from a car, usually the one with a souped-up engine and black-tinted windows. And before we are accused of being reactionary old farts, don't forget the musical battles we had to fight with our own parents who considered the New Seekers to be a little too racy.

In 2018, Emile Ratelband, a sixty-nine-year-old Dutch positivity trainer, asked a court to subtract twenty years from his legal age to reflect his young-at-heart approach to life. He protested: 'We live in a time when you can change your name and change your gender. Why can't I decide my own age? When I'm on Tinder and it says I'm sixty-nine, I don't get an answer. When I'm forty-nine with the face I have, I will be in a luxurious position.' Unsurprisingly, the court rejected his plea, ruling that it would set a dangerous precedent, not least because a thirty-five-year-old who suddenly knocked twenty years off his legal age would no longer be entitled to vote, drive, drink alcohol or get married and instead would have to return to school. However, the court did concede that 'Mr Ratelband is at liberty to feel twenty years younger than his real age and to act accordingly.' Which meant he could buy a Hawaiian shirt and matching shorts.

YOU'RE AS OLD AS YOU FEEL

So why would you want to follow a wellness programme to change your lifestyle when you're as happy as you're ever likely to be? Anyway, think for a moment of the benefits of being old and grumpy:

* Threatening to write family members out of your will carries so much more weight than sending them to their room ever did.

* You can always get a seat on public transport simply by clutching your chest and acting breathless.

* You get to dress for comfort, not fashion.

* You don't feel guilty about having an afternoon nap.

* You can blame any mood swings, irrational behaviour and controversial opinions on the side-effects of your medication.

* You get to hear your kids complain about how hard it is to be a parent.

* You can go to bed at half-past nine at night without feeling that you're missing out on life.

* You feel that you have earned the right to dispense advice to younger people, whether they want it or not.

* Your secrets are safe with your friends because they can't remember them either.

* By pretending to nod off, you can eavesdrop on other people's private conversations.

* No matter how wrong you are about something, acquaintances are reluctant to disagree with you too vehemently in case it's the last time they ever see you.

* You no longer have to pretend to like anything.

* You don't give a damn what anyone else thinks of you.

* In a hostage situation you are likely to be released first.